Director Guide

Jesus Gathers Us Together

A Psalm 23 VBS

Your VBS Dates: _____

Contents

Copyright © 2016 Concordia Publishing House
3558 S. Jefferson Ave., St. Louis, MO 63118-3968
1-800-325-3040 · www.cph.org

You can contact the Vacation Bible School team at Concordia Publishing House by email at vbsteam@cph.org.

1. Welcome to VBS!

At *Barnyard Roundup* VBS, your children learn that Jesus gathers us together! Kids want to belong, be understood, and be valued. They want a BFF at their side, no matter what! At *Barnyard Roundup*, kids will look into the Bible, God's Holy Word, to discover that Jesus is better than a BFF! Jesus, their Savior, knows them by name, rounds them up, and brings them home. He is with us always and forever—no matter what!

Psalm 23 is the Bible Memory focus of this VBS. This beloved Psalm shares our confident trust that our Lord is with us now and forever, provides all we need, and protects us. After *Barnyard Roundup*, by God's grace and through the Holy Spirit, this psalm will be in the heart and on the lips of every child, youth, and adult participating!

Each *Barnyard Roundup* day starts at Gather 'Round Opening, where the children gather with their Team Leader and the other kids in their Teams (small groups). They sing, hear God's Word, pray, see the *Opening Theme Video*, find out more about your Mission Project, and learn the day's Take-Home Point.

After the Opening, the Teams head off to five rotation sites for Storytelling, Bible Challenge, Snacks, Games, and Crafts. Finally, everyone comes back together at Gather 'Round Closing for music, prayer, and a wrap-up with the *Closing Theme Video*. Before they go, kids get a *My Shepherd Collectible* to help them share the day's theme and Bible verse with their friends and family.

VBS with Purpose—the CPH Difference

All VBS programs are not alike! So, what makes Concordia's *Barnyard Roundup* VBS different? CPH's VBS stands out because it starts with our approach to the Word of God. Every VBS lesson clearly distinguishes between God's Law and His Gospel. Children learn God's will for their lives and how the Law has been fulfilled for them in the person and work of Jesus Christ. At the center of every lesson is the Gospel: God's gracious gift of Jesus as the Savior from sin, death, and the devil.

In the crowded VBS marketplace, there is only one choice where it all comes together to faithfully teach the saving message of God's grace and mercy in Jesus Christ. After the craft glue dries, the decorations come down, and the snacks are all eaten, the only thing that matters is that the children in your VBS leave knowing their need for a Savior and that Jesus Christ alone is that Savior. And *that* is the CPH difference!

The VBS Team at Concordia Publishing House is passionate about providing you with the materials you need to carry out your VBS with purpose. Let us know how we're doing!

Your Ministry Partners,
The CPH VBS Team

Get Connected

eNewsletter
Sign up for our eNews at **vbs.cph.org** and get tips, reminders, and offers.

email
Talk to us; we are here to help at **vbsteam@cph.org**.

Facebook
Exchange ideas at **facebook.com/concordiavbs**.

Twitter
twitter.com/CPH_VBS

Pinterest
pinterest.com/CPHVBS

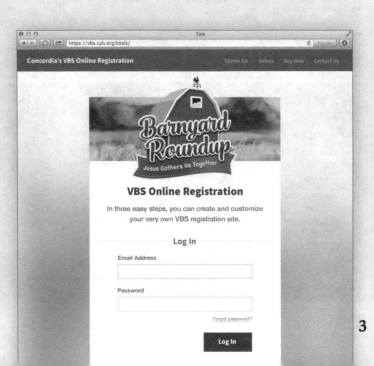

3

Lesson Summary

Key Theme:
Jesus gathers us together.

Key Bible Verses:
Psalm 23

Barnyard Roundup
Jesus Gathers Us Together

Lesson				
1		**Jesus Is the Good Shepherd** John 10:1–18	**Jesus cares, now and forever!**	**The LORD is my shepherd; I shall not want.** Psalm 23:1
2		**Jesus Feeds 5,000 People** Mark 6:30–44 John 6:1–14	**Jesus provides, now and forever!**	**He makes me lie down in green pastures.** Psalm 23:2
3		**Jesus Tells about a Sower** Matthew 13:1–23	**Jesus leads, now and forever!**	**He leads me in paths of righteousness.** Psalm 23:3
4		**Jesus Tells about a Lost Son** Luke 15:11–32	**Jesus forgives, now and forever!**	**I will fear no evil, for You are with me.** Psalm 23:4
5		**Jesus Appears to Mary in the Garden** John 20:1–18	**Jesus is our Savior, now and forever!**	**I shall dwell in the house of the LORD forever.** Psalm 23:6

Session Schedule

Barnyard Roundup activities get kids moving, engage their senses, challenge their thinking, and get them into God's Word—all so they can learn about their Savior, Jesus!

1. Start Here Together

Gather 'Round Opening (25 Minutes)

Start the day with a focus on God's Word
    and the Take-Home Point.
Teams and Team Leaders gather.
Leaders pick up supplies.
Read the Bible story. Sing and pray.
Show *Theme Video* to connect theme to real life.
Present Mission Project.
Dismiss to rotation sites.

Leader Resources

Opening/Closing Leader Guide and DVD
*Music Leader Guide with Music CD and Song-Action
DVD* (includes PowerPoints)
Mission Project Brochure
Decorations
Multimedia equipment

2. Get Moving

Barn Raising Storytelling Site (20 Minutes)

Bible story is told and kids are active!
Reinforce Take-Home Point.
Participate in small-group activity and discussion.

Leader Resources

Storytelling Leader Guide
Bible Story Posters
Elementary Student Leaflets
Team Leader Pages from *Leader Guide CD*
Leader Devotions from *Leader Guide CD*
Costumes, props, and decorations

Green Pastures Bible Challenge Site (20 Minutes)

Learn Bible Memory Verse using the following:
    Challenge activity
    Bible Memory Song
Connect to Take-Home Point and Bible story.

Leader Resources

Bible Challenge Leader Guide (with CD)
Bible Memory Verse Posters
CD player
Team Leader Pages from *Leader Guide CD*
Leader Devotions from *Leader Guide CD*

Udderly Cool Craft Site (20 Minutes)

Assemble daily craft project.
Connect to Take-Home Point and Bible story.
Listen to *Music CD*.

Leader Resources

Craft Leader Guide
Crafts and craft supplies
Music CD
Leader Devotions from *Director CD*
CD Player

Bountiful Blessings Snack Site (20 Minutes)

Make and eat yummy snacks.
Make connection with Take-Home Point.

Leader Resources

Snack Leader Guide
Snack supplies
Team Leader Pages from *Director CD*
Leader Devotions from *Director CD*

Bales of Fun Game Site (20 Minutes)

Play games.
Discuss Game Points.
Connect with Take-Home Point.

Leader Resources

Game Leader Guide
Game supplies
Game Points and Resources from *Director CD*
Team Leader Pages from *Director CD*
Leader Devotions from *Director CD*

3. End Here Together

Gather 'Round Closing (25 Minutes)

Review Take-Home Point.
Review Bible Memory Verse.
Sing and pray.
Watch *Theme Video*.
Kids receive *My Shepherd Collectibles*, local take-home
    information, and blessing from Team Leaders.

Leader Resources

Same resources as for the Opening (see above)

Starter Kit Resources

This *Director Guide* includes a *Director CD* with clip art, planning forms, charts, documents, and more—PLUS decorating images and resources.

Leader Guides with planning pages PLUS media resources!

Blue Ribbon Director Guide*
Farm-tastic Overview DVD
VBS Pastor's Overview
Big Barn Early Childhood Guide*
Good Times Music Leader Guide*
Gather 'Round Opening/Closing Leader Guide*
Barn Raising Storytelling Leader Guide*
Green Pastures Bible Challenge Leader Guide*
Udderly Cool Craft Leader Guide
Bountiful Blessings Snack Leader Guide
Bales of Fun Game Leader Guide
Youth & Adult Bible Study Flyer
Mission Project Flyer
Free Online Registration Flyer

*Includes additional CD and/or DVD content

Bible Story Posters (5, 22 x 17)
Bible Memory Posters (5, 22 x 17)
Barnyard Roundup Decorating Posters (3, 43 x 60)
Tote Bag

Samples:

Publicity Poster
Publicity Postcard
VBS Offering Envelope
Student Resources (Moovin' and Groovin' Passalong CD & DVD, My Shepherd Collectibles, Lord's House Carabiner, Farm Fresh Fun Elementary Leaflets, Little Sprouts Early Childhood Leaflets, Barn-dana Buffs Team Identifiers, Nametags 4 x 2.5)
Crafts (Psalm 23 Frame, Jesus Fish Sandart, Now & Forever Cross, Forgiven Suncatcher, Our Savior Kite)

Barnyard Roundup is faithful, fun, and flexible! The *Starter Kit* contains all the things you need to get started on your VBS adventure. Order additional resources separately so you get just the things you want.

Our website, **vbs.cph.org**, has many additional resources. Check out our Facebook page (ConcordiaVBS) to receive great ideas and support from the CPH VBS community.

VBS Comes in All Sizes!

The Small VBS = Fewer Than 50 Children

If your church has fewer than fifty kids in VBS, you'll find the site-rotation model a great fit! With site rotation, you can put everyone together, because the activities work with all ages. You don't need a class and teacher for each age group. Consider these possibilities:

- Separate children into same-age groups and rotate them through activities.

- Decide if you will include an Early Childhood site. If so, provide separate space for your Early Childhood and Elementary programs.

- Use one larger room with clearly marked sites, or put rotation sites in separate, smaller rooms.

- Keep all children together for some activities and divide into groups for others.

- Keep everyone together in one space (no need to use different areas). Each site activity happens only once, so leaders can do more than one task, especially if you have limited volunteers. One person can lead multiple components according to their interests and skills. Other adults and teens act as small-group leaders, CD & DVD operators, music leaders, action demonstrators, snack makers, or craft helpers. This on-the-job training can prepare first-time volunteers for a larger role next year.

- Some programs put preschoolers with older children, especially if there are only a few children in each age group. These situations often work well because kids know one another from other settings. Older ones enjoy helping younger ones. Young children enjoy the attention of older friends.

- Be intentional about having older children serve as leaders and helpers.

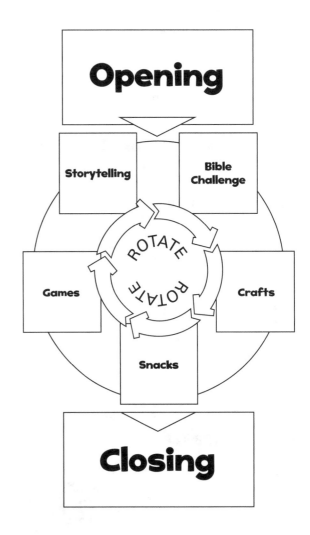

With five minutes to rotate between areas, the small-church VBS looks like this:

Time	Site
9:00–9:25	Opening
9:30–9:50	Storytelling
9:55–10:15	Bible Challenge
10:20–10:40	Snacks
10:45–11:05	Crafts
11:10–11:30	Games
11:35–12:00	Closing

The Large VBS = More Than 150 Children

One *Barnyard Roundup Starter Kit* easily accommodates an Elementary program of 150 children with five rotation sites PLUS children in a separate Early Childhood area. Over 150 elementary children? Add another set of rotation sites.

(See schedules on the *Director CD.*) Bring everyone together for the Opening and Closing events. Additional Leader Guides may be purchased separately.

Kids	Teams	Team Leaders	Rotations	Rotation Sites
1–30	1–5	1–5	1	1–5
31–150	6–25	6–25	2–5	2–5
151–300	26–50	26–50	6–10	6–10
301–450	51–75	51–75	11–15	11–15
451–600	76–100	76–100	16–20	16–20
601+	101+	101+	21+	21+

Team

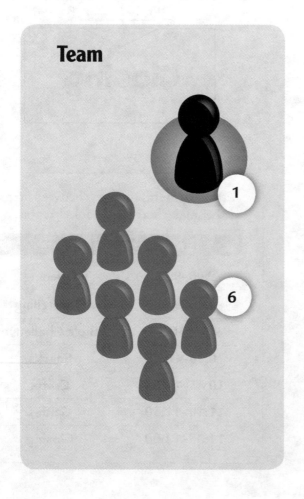

Rotation
(5 Teams)

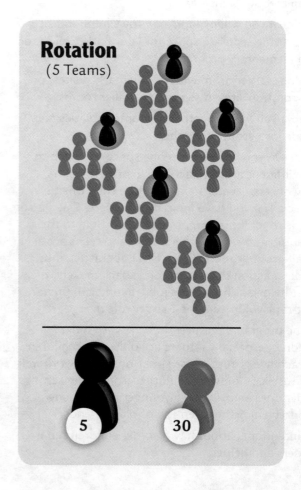

Sites and Schedules: What Fits Your VBS?

Add or Remove Sites

Some VBS Directors adjust rotation schedules to add a Music site or other activities. Others take away sites because they have less time, especially in an evening program. Feel free to make adjustments to meet your program's needs.

If you add a site to your VBS, you will be adding about twenty-five minutes of time to the schedule. If you remove a site, adjust your time by twenty-five minutes.

Flexible and Varied Schedules and Locations

Barnyard Roundup can adjust to fit your schedule. Schedules with more details for these options are on the *Director CD*. Here are some ideas:

Evening program. Add a meal and an adult Bible study. Include all groups in Opening and Closing. Cut time at Snack or Game sites.

One-day VBS. Pick stories and activities to fit your time frame.

Weekend VBS. Start on Friday evening, have sessions on Saturday, and conclude on Sunday morning.

One-hour VBS. Hold sessions over several weeks; use one lesson for two or more sessions. Choose two or three sites for each day.

All-day program. Choose two or more stories and extend Craft, Music, or Game time. Consider adding a rest period after lunch where you read one or more Christian children's books aloud.

Outdoor locations. VBS can be held outdoors at a park, in the common areas of a subdivision or housing complex, or in a backyard.

VBS Camps. How fun to take VBS to camp! Two days or five days, a camp setting provides time for growing in faith and having fun!

Schedule outlines and VBS setting options with more detail are available on the *Director CD* and at **vbs.cph.org**.

VBS for Early Childhood

Detailed Early Childhood Leader information is found in the *Early Childhood Leader Guide* (and *CD*) from the *Starter Kit*. Give this resource to your leader!

We recommend letting young children learn in their own settings and rotations. The *Early Childhood Leader Guide* has separate openings, closings, and rotation sites for young children ages 3–5 years.

Keeping young children separate from your Elementary program is beneficial for several reasons. One main one is that VBS can be a young child's first classroom experience. Parents and children may feel anxious, timid, or afraid in the midst of the hurry-flurry of a typical VBS week!

If you can, give young children separate learning spaces so that they can do age-appropriate activities with a quieter environment. Preschoolers can get lost among older kids, but in their own space, they can relax, play, and feel more secure.

Consider preschoolers' needs as you prepare their *Barnyard Roundup* VBS:

- Locate Early Childhood classrooms near restrooms and outside play areas.
- Require parents to sign children in and out.
- Use the same schedule and staff every day to provide routine and security.
- Schedule outside play in a different area or at a different time from older children.

Provide extra helpers for your Early Childhood teaching staff, following this equation:

Provide 1 leader plus 1 helper for	
3-year-olds	every 3–4 children
4-year-olds	every 4–5 children
5-year-olds	every 5–6 children

Schedule for Early Childhood

Preschoolers enjoy a variety of activities daily in large and small groups. As they arrive each day, children and parents do a brief activity together. Then children explore various interest areas. All preschoolers come together for their own Gather 'Round Opening. Afterward, they return to their class area for the Bible story and three rotation groups. From there, they move to Snacks and Games. Then they meet everyone again for their own Closing.

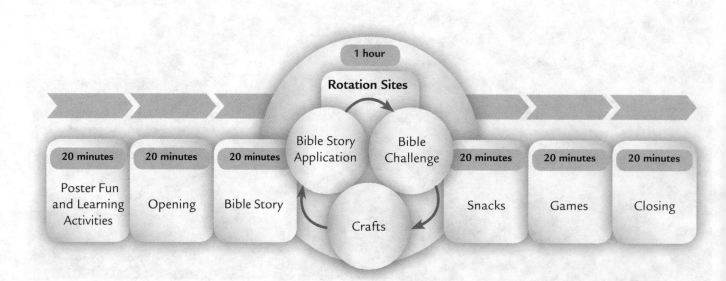

1 hour

Rotation Sites

Bible Story Application · Bible Challenge · Crafts

20 minutes	20 minutes	20 minutes		20 minutes	20 minutes	20 minutes
Poster Fun and Learning Activities	Opening	Bible Story		Snacks	Games	Closing

P23: Youth and Adult Bible Study

Appropriate for ages 12 and older, *P23: Youth and Adult Bible Study* gives youth and adults a deeper understanding of the same Bible accounts presented to the younger children. It's a great way to make VBS an intergenerational experience!

After joining the younger students for Opening, youth and adult participants move into the Bible study session. Each section of the lesson offers ideas for interactive games and activities that teenage participants may especially enjoy. If used as part of a VBS session, teens can also take part in Snacks or Crafts. Finally, youth and adult participants end their time with the younger students at Closing.

Here are some great uses for *P23: Youth and Adult Bible Study:*

- Prepare volunteers in advance for the stories they will teach.
- Use with older students. Age-appropriate activities are provided that youth will enjoy.
- Use as a Sunday School series prior to VBS to immerse your congregation in the theme.
- Offer adults a VBS class and equip them to discuss the Bible stories with their children.

This fully reproducible downloadable resource is available only online at **cph.org/P23**.

32-1665pdf   **$29.99**

Youth as VBS Volunteers

Youth have many talents and interests to share at VBS. Check out the "Recruit, Train, and Retain!" section to learn how to meaningfully involve the youth of your congregation as helpers and leaders in your VBS!

2. Director Details!

Resources for VBS Directors

The resources in this *Director Guide* and on the *Director CD* make your job easier and more satisfying. You don't have to use everything; choose resources that work best for you.

Begin VBS planning with Word and prayer. Read through Psalm 27 or Psalm 91, then pray, asking God to direct your decisions, provide willing volunteers, and give you energy to do this great work! Pray that the Holy Spirit would prepare people to hear and understand the Good News of Jesus, our Savior and Lord, and discover His plan and purpose for life. With God's Word and the materials found in *Barnyard Roundup* VBS, your team will be able to faithfully and creatively teach about Jesus, the Savior, every day!

This section will help you plan, prepare, and produce an amazing VBS for the children and volunteers at your church.

Using the Director CD

The easy-to-use disc has an automatic menu that loads when you put it in your computer's CD player. The sections of the CD match the sections of this *Director Guide*.

Director CD Contents

- Rotation Site Signs for decorating
- Forms for planning, registration, and more
- Job descriptions, charts, and forms
- Customizable postcard templates
- Decorating resources: signs, backdrop mural pattern, and other scenes
- Music resources
- Free Adobe Reader and PowerPoint Viewer programs
- Ready-to-use PowerPoint presentations. There's one for Volunteer Training and one for the Closing Celebration.
- Printable version of the *Director Guide*
- Reproducible Coloring Pages

Sample Pack Contents

Samples of student essentials and publicity resources are found in your *Starter Kit*. Order enough to get the job done!

- *Moovin' and Groovin' Passalong CD & DVD*
- Publicity/announcement postcards
- Offering envelopes
- Nametags
- *Farm Fresh Fun Elementary Leaflets*
- *Little Sprouts Early Childhood Leaflets*
- Craft samples
- *Barn-dana Buffs Team Identifiers*
- *My Shepherd Collectibles*

To order more, visit **vbs.cph.org**.

Director Job Description

- Pray for God's blessing on your Vacation Bible School and all involved.
- Partner with the Pastor and parish leaders to integrate VBS with the congregation's ministry to share the Good News of Jesus Christ with children and families.
- Oversee the "big picture."
- Manage finances and resources.
- Plan, organize, and promote VBS.
- Promote the Mission Project.
- Invite children to attend VBS.
- Order, purchase, and distribute materials and supplies; return extras.
- Recruit, train, supervise, and support volunteers.
- Delegate tasks to willing volunteers.
- Coordinate volunteers and tasks.
- Develop emergency and child-protection plans.
- Oversee and assist with publicity of VBS.
- Encourage and track registration.

- Create and maintain registration records and other details.
- Assign children and leaders to small groups.
- Provide for on-site supervision during VBS.
- Coordinate follow-up events and connections with participants.
- Create a final report for the Pastor and congregation.

MORE Resources Online at vbs.cph.org

- Free online registration tool for your church
- Easy online ordering
- Free downloads
- Clip art and other resources

Director Planning Calendar

☑️ We have your checklist!

Use this checklist or go to vbs.cph.org and download a calendar customized with dates for YOUR VBS!

Before VBS

5–6 months before VBS

☐ **Pray for VBS planning and recruitment.** Ask your Pastor to pray for VBS in worship regularly. Recruit a Prayer Coordinator and engage your church's ongoing prayer support. Ask that volunteers, VBS leaders like yourself, and children who attend would be lifted in their prayers. Keep in touch with your prayer supporters and let them know the specific needs of your volunteers and VBS.

☐ **Get to know the resources for *Barnyard Roundup*.** Review the materials in your *Starter Kit*, the CPH *2016 VBS Catalog*, or online at vbs.cph.org to understand how to use the materials. Plan any adaptations—this *Director Guide* provides suggestions!

☐ **Start reading this *Director Guide*.** Read with a pen, a highlighter, and some sticky notes to mark great ideas, highlight questions, jot down people who would be ideal for certain roles, and more! Next time you look at this *Director Guide*, you'll say, "I've done more than I thought I had!"

☐ **Start identifying and recruiting a Leadership Team.** These roles could include an Assistant Director, leaders for the sites, and a Secretary or Recruitment Coordinator. See editable job descriptions on the *Director CD*.

☐ **Learn from last year's VBS.** Review notes and reports from previous planning groups. Talk to last year's VBS leaders to get suggestions and insights.

☐ **Attend a VBS workshop with other VBS leaders.** Find out if a local church or Christian bookstore sponsors VBS workshops. Plan to attend. Often there will be free stuff and chocolate!

☐ **Write your VBS purpose statements and goals.** Talk to your Pastor about these. Give your Pastor the *Pastor's Overview* and files in the "Pastor" folder on the *Director CD*.

☐ **Choose dates; reserve space.** Add VBS dates to your church calendar, including all before- and after-VBS events. Make sure rooms and spaces are reserved.

☐ **Plan and schedule other events,** such as pre-VBS events, volunteer training and appreciation, closing programs, and a follow-up celebration.

☐ **Set your budget.** Determine how your budget is set (from church line items, donations, a special offering, registration fees, fund-raisers, etc.). Set registration fees, if required, and plan fund-raisers.

☐ **Make initial plans for using your space.** Consider alternative spaces, if needed, including outdoor locations or local schools.

☐ **Announce *Barnyard Roundup* dates** in church publications.

☐ **Check out the Mission Brochure** to find out how you can get involved with local and international missions.

4–5 months before VBS

☐ **Check in with volunteers you already recruited.** Provide resources and assistance, as needed.

☐ **Plan before and after events for *Barnyard Roundup*.**

☐ **Inform your Pastor and church staff.** Keep them up to date on the progress and needs of VBS. Let them advocate for you and the program within the congregation. Ask them to be involved during VBS so visitors can get to know them! Be sure to give your Pastor the *Pastor's Overview*.

☐ **Begin recruiting key volunteers,** including Site Leaders and a Decorating Committee.

☐ **Distribute materials to all leaders early** so they can plan and prepare ahead of time.

☐ **Develop a publicity plan with tasks and target dates.** Recruit a Publicity Coordinator, if you need one. See the job description on the *Director CD*.

☐ **Get Music resources** to people responsible for music.

☐ **Adopt recruitment strategies** that will draw children and families to your VBS. Send invitations to church children and previous VBS attendees.

☐ **Begin student registration.** Put registration and volunteer forms in church publications to begin preregistration. Explore and sign up for VBS Online Registration at vbs.cph.org.

☐ **Start registration lists.**

3–4 months before VBS

☐ **Plan your order for student resources** such as *Elementary* and *Early Childhood Leaflets*, *My Shepherd Collectibles*, *Barn-dana Buffs Team Identifiers*, and *Moovin' and Groovin' Passalong CD & DVDs*. Don't forget the crafts and decorating items! Be an early bird and beat the rush in May and June!

☐ **Encourage volunteers.** Monitor progress of the various committees or individual volunteers regularly. Establish a regular time to check in either face-to-face or via email. Offer help. Remove roadblocks. Encourage and support!

☐ **Check out ConcordiaVBS on Facebook** for great ideas and encouragement.

☐ **Communicate!** Get the word out about VBS needs, opportunities, and information. Make a sign-up poster. Use the bulletin, newsletter, emails, Facebook, webpages, word of mouth, printed invitations, and announcements from the pulpit to get the word out. And don't forget to tell your Sunday School, Day School, Midweek, and Bible study classes.

☐ **Get help!** VBS is the church's ministry. Involving others creates support as more people understand the VBS mission. Ask for help and delegate. Spread the work around!

☐ **Plan volunteer training.** Order the *VBS Tote Bags* for your volunteers to use as supply bags during VBS and as a thank-you gift.

☐ **Check on the status of fund-raisers.** Find ideas at vbs.cph.org.

2–3 months before VBS

☐ **Order student books, crafts, and follow-up materials.** Order early to make sure you get what you need. Some items cannot be reordered if stock runs out. Order online or call our great customer service center!

☐ **Purchase *Moovin' and Groovin' Passalong CD & DVDs* to hand out as kids register.** This gives them a jump on learning the songs.

☐ **Check in with volunteers and provide help, if needed.**

☐ **Continue student and volunteer recruitment and publicity efforts.**

☐ **Continue preregistration and list updates.** The online registration will download all the recruitment information into a spreadsheet! If needed, recruit additional volunteers.

☐ **Update your Pastor and church staff regularly** on the progress and needs of VBS so they can help, advise, and pray for you. Confirm the date and time of Volunteer Commissioning in the worship service and any places where they will be involved.

☐ **Begin gathering or purchasing local supplies.**

☐ **Make final space assignments.**

☐ **Decide how you will do walk-in registration and check-in at VBS.** See page 71.

1–2 months before VBS

☐ **Check progress with your volunteers.**

☐ **Check preregistration lists.**

☐ **Order or purchase materials you still need.**

☐ **Conduct volunteer training.** Hand out resources. Share plans for all VBS events, including volunteer commissioning.

☐ **Review and update safety procedures and emergency plans.**

☐ **Relax and enjoy!** Take a look back and see all that has been accomplished by God's grace, mercy, and blessing! Praise and thank our mighty God! Lift up your needs to Him!

2–4 weeks before VBS

☐ **Check preregistration lists.** Order additional student materials and recruit additional volunteers as needed.

☐ **Finalize plans for volunteer appreciation.**

☐ **Finalize plans for VBS events** and follow-up plans with your Pastor and church staff.

☐ **Check the progress of site volunteers regularly.**

1–2 weeks before VBS

☐ **Acknowledge and pray for VBS volunteers** in a worship service. A Volunteer Commissioning is included on the *Director CD*.

☐ **Distribute supplies and equipment.**

☐ **Decorate and set up your space.**

☐ **Prepare lists, signs, welcome letters, and other materials for registration.** Set up the registration area. Use the Table Banner provided in the *Starter Kit*.

☐ **Make nametags for volunteers and kids.**

☐ **Check and replenish the first-aid kit.** Make sure safety and emergency plans are in place.

☐ **Relax and enjoy.** Plan how you will take time to enjoy the week and all that God is accomplishing through His Word and your efforts! God will bless your VBS!

During VBS

Do these things every day:

- **Pray, encourage, inform.** Gather staff before the daily openings to pray, make announcements, share needs, and hear concerns. Ask Site Teams to meet and check plans for the next day.

- **Make sure all volunteers have arrived.** Find substitutes or be ready to step in if needed. Some Directors recruit "floaters" to step in as substitutes and extra hands.

- **Welcome children and families.** Get plenty of volunteers to help with first-day registration, using the procedures described in the registration section of this *Director Guide*.

- **Check in with registration and address questions from volunteers and parents.** This is especially important the first couple of days at VBS!

- **Make sure all children are signed in and out** by their own parents or by people authorized by the parents.

- **Join Opening and Closing activities.** Get to know the children and their parents.

- **Send information home** about your program, Mission Project, and Closing Program.

- **Spread VBS joy!** Visit sites, greet families and children, and encourage volunteers.

- **Observe and guide volunteers.** Anticipate problems and preempt them. Provide guidance and advice for struggling leaders.

- **Check attendance.**

- **Collect offerings.**

- **Support volunteers.** Check in on sites to encourage leaders and children.

- **Thank volunteers.** Appreciative words, small gifts, notes, and prayer show volunteers your care for them. See pages 51–52 for ideas.

- **Be available.** Leaders may need guidance and help with discipline and child control. Be ready and able to step in and assist or take the lead, if necessary. Have a support plan for yourself with a Pastor and with church leadership.

- **Coordinate health concerns.** Some children have allergies or special needs. Work with the Snack Leader and other leaders to accommodate the needs in a discreet and confidential way.

- **Put out fires.** Work with volunteers, parents, and church leaders to address their concerns and frustrations.

- **Make announcements.** Remind children of the mission offering and other information.

- **Tend to injuries.** Prepare a first-aid kit, keep it close at hand, and have emergency contact information recorded and easily accessible for all children and adults in your VBS. Have a list of local emergency numbers on hand. Keep important information on a clipboard to travel with you for easy reference.

Do these things sometime during the VBS week:

- **Prepare Attendance Certificates and Volunteer Certificates** or gifts for volunteers to give on the last day or at the Closing Program. See the gift suggestions in this *Director Guide*. Certificates are in the folder on the *Director CD*.

- **Document.** Items to add to your clipboard for convenience include Team assignments, room assignments, complete registration, emergency contacts, and the week-at-a-glance schedule. In addition, be sure to be prepared to collect and document supply requests; prayer requests; comments from volunteers, parents, and church workers; and general observations for improvement.

- **Distribute the *Passalong CD & DVD*s.** We recommend purchasing one per family to give out at registration or some other time during the week. This is the longest-lasting memento you can give your VBS families. Kids will sing these songs for years to come, and it may be the only connection unchurched children have to God's Word.

- **Invite parents and friends to a Closing Celebration Program.** Share photos of the week in a PowerPoint slide show. Sing favorite songs; recite Bible Memory Verses and Take-Home Points. Find an outline for a Closing Program with correlating PowerPoint slides on the *Director CD*. As you finalize Closing Program plans, notify volunteers of any changes.

- **Invite children and families to follow-up activities.** Keep reaching out to attendees and newcomers with follow-up activities.

- **Give volunteers the CPH online evaluation survey.** Ask volunteers to fill out our evaluation survey (cph.org/vbsfeedback). We want to hear from you!

1–2 Weeks after VBS

- **Help returning visitors feel at home.** Display the week's decorations, crafts, photos, and student projects for a few weeks after VBS. Members will enjoy seeing these too!
- **Gather and store supplies;** return any borrowed items.
- **Evaluate your VBS.** Discuss successes and opportunities for improvement with your volunteers. Record all comments and ideas for use next year.
- **Make a final report.** Include statistics on expenses, attendance, and food and supply amounts, as well as ideas for improvements.
- **Finish notes for next year.** Insert publicity pieces, reports, and any other pertinent information in this workbook for next year's planners.
- **Continue communication.** Mail postcards or letters to children and families who attended and invite them to worship services, Sunday School, Midweek programs, and other church activities.
- **Share your *Barnyard Roundup* results** with your congregation, administrative boards, and church staff. Provide your Pastor and evangelism committee with information about families who are interested in your church. Get started on your follow-up events and strategies.
- **If written, send evaluation surveys to Concordia Publishing House;** or remind volunteers to fill out evaluation surveys online at cph.org/vbsfeedback.

Gather This Great Idea!

The *Director CD* has a customizable version of this Planning Calendar. Enter your VBS date, and your dates for these steps will be auto-populated.

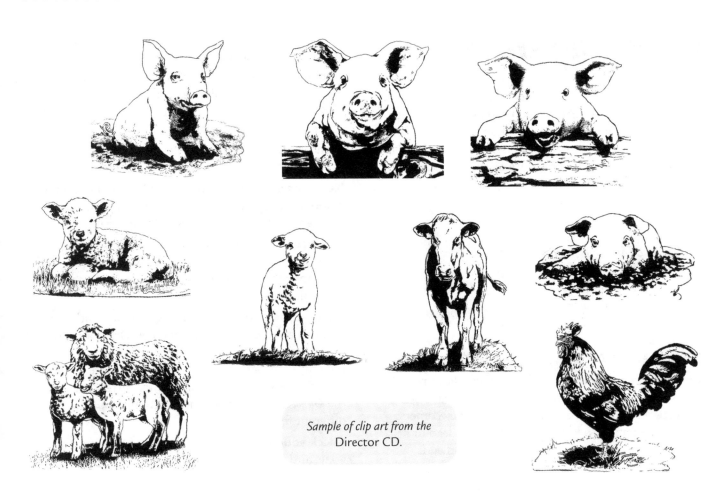

Sample of clip art from the Director CD.

3. Plan!

Choosing Dates

Selecting your VBS dates is a very important task. Each community has scheduling challenges. Consider the people you hope to reach as you explore alternatives. List schedule conflicts or concerns on the Choose Dates Form on the *Director CD*. List your top three date options, then choose a final date as soon as possible so people can avoid making other plans that conflict with VBS.

Gather This Great Idea!
When determining your VBS dates, use the Choose Dates Form found on the *Director CD*. There are lots of other helpful forms on the *CD* too!

Issues to Consider as You Choose Dates

Church staff availability. It is vital that your Pastor and staff have visibility with children and parents and opportunities to develop connections with newcomers. Ask staff members to lead worship or music, lead or help with a site, or greet families as VBS begins and ends.

Local school schedule. Some school districts offer summer school. Avoid scheduling during your district's summer school. If your community has year-round schools, offer VBS during one or more of the breaks.

Community conflicts. Consider scheduled community events such as swimming lessons, sports camps, and scout camps. Call other congregations to avoid scheduling VBS at the same time.

Weather concerns. If possible, avoid scheduling during traditionally hot or wet weeks.

New program invitations. Schedule VBS about a month before fall programs kick off so you can promote those programs in follow-up phone calls and visits.

Work and child-care needs. To get more children to attend, consider an all-day program or free transportation. Make sure you have nursery care available for volunteers.

Alternatives. Provide an evening program with a meal to allow families to attend together. Other alternatives might include a one-day, all-day VBS or one day or evening each week for five weeks. Make sure to consider how different schedules might affect attendance. Check the *Director CD* for more information about these different formats.

Check yourself. Choose options that best meet your goals and intentions for VBS.

Space

Space informs many decisions. Sketch your facility, showing locations for every site and Early Childhood room. On the *Director CD*, there is a Space Plan Diagram. Make space assignments for the entire week so each area is set up only once. Consider the needs of all levels.

Gather This Great Idea!

Use the Space Plan Diagram on the *Director CD* to help you consider space needs.

Early Childhood Space Needs

Preschoolers feel safe and secure with few disruptions and limited time outside of their main space. Rooms with child-size tables and chairs that are close to restrooms and an outdoor play area are ideal. Make sure you have areas available for the variety of activities scheduled.

An Opening and Closing area where all preschoolers can gather together is necessary if you have more than one Early Childhood room. Leaders need a CD player and electrical access.

Gather This Great Idea!

Gather all children together for openings and closings. Then you'll need only one *Polly the Pig Puppet*, instead of one for every Early Childhood group.

Elementary Space Needs

This VBS is designed in the popular site-rotation model. The elementary children start the day together at Opening. They gather at the end for Closing in the same space. Space is needed for the following sites: Storytelling, Bible Challenge, Games, Snacks, and Crafts.

Each site has its own unique space and supply requirements. For more information, consult the section called "Sites!" beginning on page 23 of this *Director Guide*. Use your largest space for Opening and Closing because elementary kids, youth, and adults meet together. You also need to use multimedia equipment there to show the *Theme Videos*, the *Song-Action DVD*, and PowerPoint presentations.

Sites should be located far enough apart to avoid distractions. Two sites that can be located at opposite ends of the same large area together are Crafts and Snacks. The Crafts and Bible Challenge sites need places to plug in CD players. If possible, locate Games outdoors on grass. Playgrounds may distract from the organized games.

Consider any additional spaces needed, such as a volunteer's hospitality area; a supply center; areas for registration, attendance, and award tracking; and any food service needs for snacks.

Youth and Adult Space Needs

If your VBS includes youth or adult classes, consider the best space for them to do their Bible study. Talk to your youth and adult leaders to find out what they prefer. Some leaders prefer less formal space, like a room with couches and chairs; others prefer tables and chairs.

Budget

Vacation Bible School is a big event at any church. It takes a commitment of people and financial resources to offer a quality program. Begin by determining a budget based on cost per child. Include all costs: curriculum, decorating, food, and any other expenses. Consider how to meet financial challenges. Start a list of needs and wishes. Track your resources with the VBS Budget Worksheet on the *Director CD*. The budget worksheet will automatically calculate costs.

Start by listing all sources of income. Then flip through the *2016 VBS Catalog* and write items you need and want on your Needs and Wishes List, even if you think you can't afford them right now. Add costs beside each item, then add up costs and transfer them to the Budget Worksheet. Remember to add costs for copies, craft supplies, snacks, postage, publicity, and volunteer appreciation.

> *Gather This Great Idea!*
> Use the VBS Budget Worksheet on the *Director CD* to track your resources.

Common Income Sources

Church budgets. Many churches cover some or all VBS expenses in their congregational budget. Others offset costs with donations, registration fees, sponsorships, or fund-raising. If you need to generate funds, start early to meet your goals.

Registration fees. Some congregations have strong feelings about not charging for outreach or educational programs such as VBS. Others find that parents are accustomed to paying fees for their children's activities and programs, so a registration fee is not limiting. To make sure no one is left out, many Directors work with a maximum cost per family or offer scholarships. Ask your church staff and key leaders for their perspectives as you decide which options to use.

Sponsor a child. Many churches give members an opportunity to sponsor a child's week. After you've done your budget, figure out a cost per child and give church members the opportunity to contribute that amount to send a child to VBS. Use the Sponsor Letter and Sponsor Certificate to recruit and thank your benefactors (on *Director CD*).

Sponsor a site. Ask church members to sponsor their favorite VBS site. Figure out the costs of leader and student resources for each site to set a sponsorship price. Thank site sponsors in the same ways you recognize those who sponsor children.

Seek donations. Take a special VBS offering at church, or ask church groups, such as Bible classes or the men's or women's groups, to donate for VBS. Visit the groups to share your VBS purpose and goals so they understand how VBS fits into your church's mission.

Fund-raisers for VBS are growing in popularity. Old standards like car washes, bake sales, ice cream socials, and silent auctions do work! Use the fund-raiser event to promote the theme and dates of your VBS. Encourage people to preregister at your event.

Give thanks. Publicly thank donors and sponsors by listing names in bulletins and newsletters. Post pictures of your VBS on a bulletin board during and after VBS and add a thank-you note for all.

> *Gather This Great Idea!*
> Use the Sponsor Letter and Sponsor Certificate to recruit and thank your benefactors (*Director CD*).

More Budget-Stretching Ideas

- **Coordinate your VBS with other congregations.** Work with one or create a co-op with a network of other churches. Work together to create decorating items and props for Storytelling. (Coordinating your dates is important for this to work!) Share Bible costumes, game equipment, and other VBS needs.

- **Ask local businesses to donate** cups, drinks, or other supplies. Call or use the Business Sponsor Letter on the *Director CD*.

- **Ask individuals for their support.** Use the Sponsor Letter on the *Director CD*. Some individuals love to sponsor the purchase of the *Collectibles* or the *Passalong CD & DVD*, a *Barnyard Roundup* Craft item, a special snack, or a giant inflatable for games or a special celebration event.

- **Acknowledge donations** in letters to families and in Closing Program bulletins. Send thank-you letters after VBS to let them know how the donations helped. Include highlights of your program.

- **List snack and craft needs** on Supply Request Tags, found on the *Director CD*. Hang the tags on a display in your entry. Ask people to take tags and return them with the requested item to a collection box near the display.

- **Order VBS resources early.** Some items can't be reordered if they run out, leaving you to find a costly substitute. Remember, Concordia Publishing House will give a full refund on materials returned in saleable condition and in a timely way.

Gather This Great Idea!

List snack and craft needs on Supply Request Tags, found on the *Director CD*.

The Role of Your Pastor

The primary roles of your Pastor are to preach God's Word, administer the Sacraments, and serve the congregation as he teaches, guards, and cares for the people. Pastors aren't called to be secretaries, janitors, CEOs, or a VBS's jack-of-all-trades—but sometimes they do that stuff!

As VBS Director, talk with your Pastor about VBS. Ask your Pastor to share his perspective on VBS and how he will serve in this ministry. If you have specific needs or concerns about VBS, share those with him. Provide him with information about VBS. Give your Pastor the *Pastor's Overview* from the *Starter Kit*. This resource shares the purpose of VBS, the themes and Bible accounts, the resources available in the *Director Guide* that specifically apply to Pastors, and the resources *Barnyard Roundup VBS* offers. Be sure to give the resource a quick read before you pass it on! Also share the resources in the "Pastor" folder on the *Director CD* with your Pastor.

To keep your Pastor up to date on the progress of VBS, ask if you can schedule a few regular meetings with him during the VBS planning time. In those meetings, reflect with your Pastor on the work being done to achieve the purpose of the ministry of VBS in your congregation. Share your thanksgiving for God's provision as well as your current needs, prayer concerns, answered prayers, and plans for reaching out to kids and families from the community. Review the schedule, including the places where VBS will be part of the worship of the congregation. Update your Pastor on "new to VBS" volunteers, and share their God-given gifts. VBS is often a starting place for service in other ministries.

May God richly bless your partnership with your Pastor!

VBS Mission Project

Mission projects provide a way to teach young people to respond to God's love by sharing the gifts He gives. Collecting money or items needed for a specific mission project gives children a tangible way to respond to the love of God and serve their neighbor.

Through our Mission Project, *Tin Roofs for Africa*, we'll gather together offerings to show the love and mercy of Christ by providing tin and other supplies for Lutheran church roofs in Africa. Then men, women, and children can have a better place to worship God and learn about the amazing love of Jesus—rain or shine! Specifically, our offering can provide tin for the roofs, wood for the church structure, nails, and toolboxes with hammers, saws, and other tools!

Our mission partner is The Lutheran Church—Missouri Synod.

Sharing the Project at VBS

The Mission Brochure in the *Starter Kit* and the five videos on the *Opening/Closing DVD* explain how this project will share God's love and mercy in Christ with children and families. Show the *Mission Project Videos* during Opening to enlist the support of children, parents, and church members. The Opening Leader can offer a prayer asking God to bless these offerings and the service through the work of *Tin Roofs for Africa*. Also, check out the project website, lcms.org/tinroofs, for the most current resources.

Mission Project poster. The details for the Mission Project are in the brochure in the *Starter Kit*. The brochure opens up into a poster you can use to track the gifts given.

Mission Project display. Share information, inspire, and show current offerings with a *Tin Roofs for Africa* display. See the photographs on page 39 for examples. See additional instructions in the *Decorating Videos* on the *Farm-tastic Overview DVD* and detailed description on the *Director CD*. This is a great place to display the poster. Locate your display near your Opening Site or wherever you feature this Mission Project. Our icons (church, wooden structure, nails, toolbox, and piece of tin) are available on the *Director CD* for use with your project.

Keep track of offerings. Use the poster to keep track of offerings and visually illustrate gifts you have received.

Submit your gift. A submission form is located in the brochure. A prepaid envelope for this specific project is inserted in the brochure. Complete the form and send it with your gift in the envelope provided. Make your check payable to The Lutheran Church—Missouri Synod, and include IM0016MKXVBH000 on your check memo line for proper credit to this project.

If you misplace the form and envelope, send offerings to The Lutheran Church—Missouri Synod, P.O. Box 66861, St. Louis, MO 63166-6861. Include the congregation or group name, contact person name, address, city, state, phone, email, and project codes IM0016MKXVBH000 and A16155-61045.

The two codes and the P.O. Box 66861 are specific to this project and are very important. They get your gift to the right place!

To make a credit card gift, call our donor care line at 888-930-4438 or make your gift online at lcms.org/tinroofs.

4. Sites!

Concordia's VBS is designed using the site-rotation model. The elementary children start the day together at Opening. They gather at the end for Closing in the same space. In between, the children rotate to five sites (Storytelling, Bible Challenge, Games, Snacks, and Crafts) with their Teams (small groups of six students and a leader). See the following pages for all the details you need to know about each site.

Kids	Teams	Team Leaders	Rotations	Rotation Sites
1–30	1–5	1–5	1	1–5
31–150	6–25	6–25	2–5	2–5
151–300	26–50	26–50	6–10	6–10
301–450	51–75	51–75	11–15	11–15
451–600	76–100	76–100	16–20	16–20
601+	101+	101+	21+	21+

Team

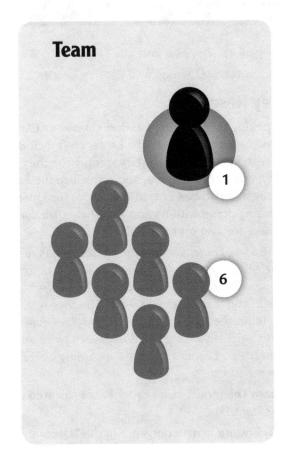

Rotation
(5 Teams)

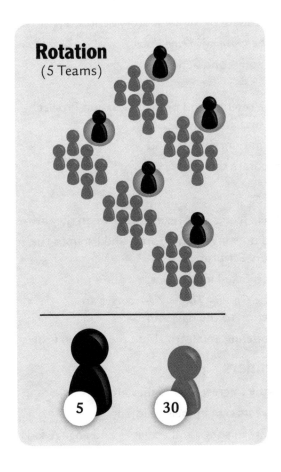

Gather 'Round Opening

Why Gather 'Round Opening and Closing?

Your kids will love to gather 'round at the beginning of your VBS to find out about the "farm-tastic" activities in store for them. VBS starts and ends with everyone gathered at the cross to hear God's Holy Word and learn of His plan and purpose for us. The Teams gather at VBS Opening to connect, check in, pray, and sing praise to God. Everyone is introduced to the day's Bible account, the Take-Home Point, and Bible Memory Verse. They "jump in" to the experience of VBS!

Oh come, let us worship and bow down; let us kneel before the LORD, our Maker! Psalm 95:6

Site Summary

Your VBS time dawns with Gather 'Round Opening each day! Children sing, pray, are introduced to the Bible story and the Take-Home Point, view the *Theme Video*, and watch the *Mission Project Video*. Detailed instructions for this site are included in the *Opening & Closing Leader Guide*.

The Opening Leader

- introduces the Take-Home Point and the Bible story;
- leads a reading of the Bible story Scripture;
- shows the *Opening Theme Video*;
- teaches songs and actions;
- prays;
- takes the offering and presents Mission Project information and video;
- makes announcements; and
- may decorate this site.

Children

- meet their Teams and Team Leader when they arrive;
- sing and do song actions, pray, and listen to the Bible story Scripture;
- speak the Take-Home Point;
- watch the *Opening Theme Video* to get an introduction to the day; and
- give an offering and learn about the Mission Project.

Team Leaders

- arrive early to greet kids as they arrive;
- have parents sign in their children;
- participate in songs and activities and engage kids to do the same;

- pick up supplies; and
- assist the Opening and Closing Leader, as needed.

Key Resources

Opening and Closing Leader: *Opening & Closing Leader Guide with Leader DVD*. The *Leader DVD* includes *Theme Videos*. These ten video skits identify the theme for the day, relate it to real life, and introduce the Take-Home Points. It also has PowerPoint slides for Opening and Closing presentations and song lyrics. *Mission Project Videos* are also on this DVD.

The *Music Leader Guide (with 2-Disc Set)* has resources for the Music Leader, including Music Scores for the theme songs. The *Music CD* includes audio files with both vocal and instrumental tracks. The *Song-Action DVD* includes the *Song-Action Videos*, *Song Lyric PowerPoints* with lyrics only, *Song Lyric Videos* with lyrics and music, and Music Leader resources, including lead sheets for theme songs.

Team Leaders: Team Leader Pages (located on the *Director CD*)

Decorating instructions are in the "Decorate!" section of this *Director Guide*.

Gather 'Round Closing

Site Summary

The Closing ends the day with singing, praying, seeing a *Theme Video*, reviewing the Bible Memory Verse, and communicating your local VBS announcements.

The Closing Leader

- teaches the daily themes using the *Music CD*;
- reviews the Bible story and Take-Home Point;
- shows the *Theme Video*;
- reviews the Bible Memory Verse;
- prays and makes announcements;
- hands out the *My Shepherd Collectibles* and take-home information to children; and
- decorates this site (with the Opening Leader) and other helpers.

Children

- sing, do song actions, pray, and respond to Take-Home Points;
- hear about the Mission Project;
- review Bible Memory Verse;
- watch the *Closing Theme Video*; and
- receive *My Shepherd Collectibles* and take-home information.

Team Leaders

- participate in songs and activities and encourage kids to join in;
- assist Closing Leader in distributing *My Shepherd Collectibles* and take-home information;
- have parents sign out their children; and
- return unused supplies or containers so they can be refilled for the next day.

Key Resources

- **Closing Leader:** *Opening & Closing Leader Guide with Leader DVD* and *Music Leader Guide (with 2-Disc Set)*, invitation to Closing Program, Parent Letter, and Mission Project information (*Leader DVD*)
- **Children:** *My Shepherd Collectibles*
- **Team Leaders:** Team Leader Pages (located on the *Director CD*)
- **Decorating instructions** are in the "Decorate!" section of this *Director Guide*.

Storytelling— Barn Raising Storytelling

Why Barn Raising Storytelling?

In Barn Raising Storytelling, children learn that Jesus gathers us together. Now and forever, Jesus cares for us, provides for all our needs, leads us, and forgives us. Jesus is our Savior!

Gather the people to Me, that I may let them hear My words, so that they may learn to fear Me all the days that they live on the earth, and that they may teach their children so. Deuteronomy 4:10

Site Summary

Children hear God's Word and actively participate in the Bible storytelling. With their teams, they discuss and discover what the Bible story means for them. Detailed instructions for this site are included in the *Barn Raising Storytelling Leader Guide*.

The Storyteller

- decorates this site, possibly with the help of others;
- greets kids to start this site's experiences;
- directs and leads Bible storytelling activities that involve every child;
- shares the Take-Home Point; and
- supervises the Teams as they discuss the Bible story and do *Farm Fresh Fun Elementary Leaflet* activities.

Children

- actively help tell the Bible stories;
- respond to Take-Home Points; and
- participate in storytelling activities.

Team Leaders

- get involved in the storytelling, encouraging their Teams to participate as well;
- use Team Leader Pages to lead their Team in "Talk It Over" discussions;
- help children read and do *Farm Fresh Fun Elementary Leaflet* activities; and
- assist the Storyteller, as needed.

Key Resources

Storyteller: *Barn Raising Storytelling Leader Guide*

Children: *Farm Fresh Fun Elementary Leaflets*

Team Leaders: Team Leader Pages (*Storytelling CD* or *Director CD*)

Decorating instructions are in the "Decorate!" section of this *Director Guide*.

Bible Challenge— Green Pastures Bible Challenge

Why Green Pastures Bible Challenge?

Bible Challenge is the place where the Teams explore, learn, and remember the Bible Memory Verse for each lesson. After VBS is over, God's powerful and gracious Word remains in their hearts, minds, and ultimately in their lives. First, there is an activity to connect the Bible verse content with the kids' lives today. Then, the kids learn the Bible Memory Song.

Why a song? God made our minds to hold on to words and concepts set to music! Stories and Scripture have long been remembered through song. VBS is using that amazing, God-created process!

May our gracious God bless you as you share God's Word with the Teams in VBS!

Let the word of Christ dwell in you richly, teaching and admonishing one another in all wisdom, singing psalms and hymns and spiritual songs, with thankfulness in your hearts to God. Colossians 3:16

Site Summary

Children meet in Teams for an exciting Challenge Activity and song to help them remember God's Word! Detailed instructions for this site are included in the *Green Pastures Bible Challenge Leader Guide.*

The Bible Challenge Leader

- decorates this site, possibly with the help of others;
- leads Bible Challenge Activities with the support of the Team Leaders;
- shares the Take-Home Point; and
- teaches the Bible Memory Verse with a song and actions.

Children

- respond to Take-Home Point;
- engage in Bible Challenge Activities, which include hands-on learning; and
- learn Bible Memory Songs and actions.

Team Leaders

- lead Bible Challenge Activities with their Teams;
- participate in the songs and activities that teach Bible Memory Verses; and
- assist the Bible Challenge Leader, as needed.

Key Resources

- **Bible Challenge Leader:** *Green Pastures Bible Challenge Leader Guide (with CD), Bible Memory Verse Posters*
- **Decorating instructions** are in the "Decorate!" section of this *Director Guide.*

Games—Bales of Fun Games

Why Bales of Fun Games?

Life on a farm is hard work and lots of fun too! There's so much to do—animals to play with, jumping in the hay, hiking, and maybe riding on a tractor! It's a place to use the strength and skill of the bodies God has created and blessed! God created His kids for an active life! Bales of Fun Games provides activity with purpose as the games reinforce the experience of VBS!

May our almighty God give you strength, stamina, and joy as the Teams come to play!

Every athlete exercises self-control in all things. They do it to receive a perishable wreath, but we an imperishable.
1 Corinthians 9:25

Site Summary

Children play games that reinforce the Bible story and Take-Home Point. Detailed instructions for this site are included in the *Bales of Fun Game Leader Guide*.

The Game Leader

- gives game instructions and supervises games with the Game Team;
- may decorate this site, possibly with help from others;
- shares the Take-Home Point; and
- helps kids discuss Game Points and discover the Bible-story connections.

Children

- respond to Take-Home Points;
- have a blast as they play games that reinforce the Take-Home Point and Bible story; and
- discuss Game Points to find Bible-story connections and catch their breath.

Team Leaders

- participate in games and cheer on all the Teams;
- discuss Game Points on the Team Leader Pages to find Bible-story connections;
- listen carefully to the Game Leader's instructions and help kids play; and
- assist Game Leader, as needed.

Key Resources

- **Game Leader:** *Bales of Fun Game Leader Guide*, game supplies
- **Decorating suggestions** are listed in the *Leader Guide*.

Snacks—Bountiful Blessings Snacks

Why Bountiful Blessings Snacks?

A farm is an active place, and kids get hungry! Bountiful Blessings Snacks will be a favorite place for nourishment, conversation, and connections. Mealtimes for Christians are always a great time for prayer, conversation, and growing in faith and fellowship. At Snacks, Teams have a chance to "gather 'round" and get to know one another over the delicious snack of the day. If you've done one VBS or twenty, you know that VBS "runs on its stomach"!

Blessings to you as you share the gift of food and hospitality with VBS kids and leaders!

Jesus said to them, "I am the bread of life; whoever comes to Me shall not hunger, and whoever believes in Me shall never thirst." John 6:35

Site Summary

Make and eat snacks that reinforce the Bible story or Take-Home Points. Detailed instructions for this site are included in the *Bountiful Blessings Snack Leader Guide*.

The Snack Leader

- may decorate this site, possibly with the help of others;
- introduces snacks, reviews Bible stories, and shares Take-Home Points;
- leads a daily snack prayer or asks others to do so; and
- gives instructions for children to make their own snacks.

Children

- respond to Take-Home Points;
- make and eat theme-related snacks that reinforce the Bible story or Take-Home Point; and
- clean up their area and assist with other tasks.

Team Leaders

- hand out supplies and assist Snack Leader, as needed;
- help kids make and eat their snacks; and
- clean and sanitize behind children.

Key Resources

- **Snack Leader:** *Bountiful Blessings Snack Leader Guide* and snack supplies
- **Decorating instructions** are in the "Decorate!" section of this *Director Guide*.

Crafts—Udderly Cool Crafts

Why Udderly Cool Crafts?

God has created us, His people, to create, to remember our God and His Word, to praise our God, and to share with others the Good News that Jesus, our Savior, gathers us together. One of the favorite sites of VBS is Crafts, where kids and adults use their God-given creative gifts to remember God's presence and promises.

Blessings to you as you provide these creative moments and memories for VBS kids and leaders!

Let every skillful craftsman among you come and make all that the LORD has commanded. Exodus 35:10

Site Summary

Children make crafts that reinforce the Bible story, Take-Home Point, or Bible Memory Verse. Detailed instructions for this site are included in the *Udderly Cool Craft Leader Guide.*

The Craft Leader

- reviews Bible stories and shares Take-Home Points;
- makes and shows sample crafts;
- introduces crafts and gives written and spoken instructions;
- engages kids in dialogue about how the craft connects to the Bible story;
- plays the *Moovin' and Groovin' Passalong CD & DVD* while children make crafts; and
- may decorate this site, possibly with the help of others.

Children

- make crafts that reinforce the Bible stories, memory verses, or Take-Home Points;
- respond to Take-Home Points;
- discuss Bible story connections as they work;
- listen to VBS songs as they create; and
- help clean up.

Team Leaders

- hand out supplies and assist the Craft Leader, as needed;
- listen carefully to Craft Leader instructions so they can assist children; and
- help clean up.

Key Resources

- **Craft Leader:** *Udderly Cool Craft Leader Guide, Moovin' and Groovin' Passalong CD & DVD*, CD player, supplies (Crafts sold separately.)
- **Decorating instructions** are in the "Decorate!" section of this *Director Guide.*

Music—Good Times Music

Why Good Times Music?

For thousands of years, the people of God have used music to sing God's Word and praise His name and mighty deeds. VBS is a great place for kids to gather to sing praise to our triune God—Father, Son, and Holy Spirit—who has delivered us through the person and work of the Son, Jesus Christ.

Make a joyful noise to the LORD, all the earth; break forth into joyous song and sing praises! Psalm 98:4

Site Summary

Some churches include a Music site as part of the daily rotations in addition to the music in the openings and closings. Children learn the VBS songs and actions and enjoy the opportunity to express their faith with music and movements. The *Good Times Music Leader Guide (with 2-Disc Set)* makes it easy to add a Music site! Other churches simply weave the VBS music into all the sites. The *Good Times Music Leader Guide (with 2-Disc Set)* will help you with whatever model you choose!

Music, Music, Music!

- **The *Good Times Music Leader Guide (with 2-Disc Set)*** comes in your *Starter Kit*. The *2-Disc Set* features a *Music CD* with eight songs in two versions—one with lyrics and one with accompaniment only. The five Bible Memory Songs are also included. The second disc is the *Song-Action DVD*. In addition to the eight *Song-Action Videos*, this disc includes *Song Lyric PowerPoints* with lyrics only and *Song Lyric Videos* with lyrics and music. The *Good Times Music Leader Guide* has accompaniment scores with guitar chords.

- **Recorded music is not reproducible**, so share music with *Moovin' and Groovin' Passalong CD & DVD*s. The CD and DVD set provides ALL the VBS music recordings on a CD and the *Song-Action Videos* on a DVD. We recommend getting one for every family. Give them out at registration or as a souvenir after VBS. This may be the only connection unchurched children have to God's Word. All children will enjoy singing and dancing to these songs for years to come. We promise!

- **Questions?** Contact Concordia's Copyright Office at 1-800-325-0191 or copyrights@cph.org.

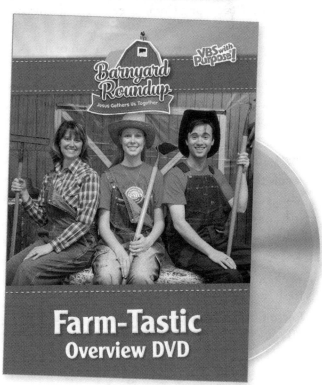

5. Decorate!

Decorating Basics

Decorating creates an exciting environment for children to learn in. Decorating is easy-breezy as you show and share the *Barnyard Roundup* theme and its message that "Jesus gathers us together."

Jump in and decorate your place with hay bales, barn exteriors and interiors, wooden fences, wheelbarrows, pigpens, chicken coops, cornfields, sunflower patches, farm animals, blue sky, and sunsets. Round up lots of farm-tastic VBS fun!

The *Director CD* has PDFs of decorating resources, line art of theme/backdrop images, Site Signs, clip art, and other resources that make decorating fun and easy. Our *Decorating Videos* show decorating sets and objects being made. Find these on the *Farm-tastic Overview DVD* and at vbs.cph.org. *Leader CDs* also include clip art and line art as well as DIY directions and templates for that specific site in their "Decorating Resources" folder. Check out our Pinterest page and Facebook for more ideas from us and other VBS leaders.

Recruit a Decorating Crew

- Recruit a Decorating Committee to transform your space.
- List the names and contact information of decorating volunteers on the Decorating Committee Form on the *Director CD*.
- Recruit a Decorating Coordinator; use the job description on the *Director CD*.
- Let the coordinator recruit helpers to plan and decorate.
- Involve people in decorating who can't help during VBS.
- Ask congregation members with artistic talents to volunteer.
- Ask youth to create decorations and set up.
- Look outside the usual choices of volunteers for fresh, new people and ideas.
- Recruit helpers to move furniture on the day before VBS.

Gather This Great Idea!

The *2016 VBS Catalog* has many decorating resources to help you, including the huge *Barnyard Roundup Decorating Posters*. Among our favorites are the *Mounting Tabs*, the *Hanger Pole*, and the *Hanging Hooks*! Our stand-up collection features a life-size figure of Jesus and a cross.

Assess Your Space

One of the decorator's first tasks is to take a critical look at the facility. Is it inviting and appropriate for children? Every site has challenges, but you can transform yours into a welcoming place for children and parents.

- **First things first: Jesus is central.** Use decorations as a backdrop to enhance the environment and teach the truth about Jesus Christ. Seek ways to visually point children to Jesus, their Savior. Decorate with Storytelling areas in mind to embed the visuals of the daily Bible stories in your decorations. Consider using the life-size *Jesus Stand-Up* in your environment. Add sheep from the huge *Decorating Posters* for Jesus, our Good Shepherd.
- **Clean up.** Move out or hide excess and inappropriate items and junk. Clean all areas.
- **Size it up.** Use furniture that is appropriate for the various sizes of children.
- **Hit the floor.** The floor is a decorator's canvas too! Use gingham tablecloths, rugs, and tarps to clearly define and identify where students should sit in each site.
- **Label it.** Make signs for the Registration area, Early Childhood rooms, Opening, and restrooms. Use Site Signs (*Director CD*) to identify sites and Early Childhood rooms. Post names of leaders and helpers with their sites.
- **Double up.** Place signs at eye level for children. Help adults find locations in registration crowds by hanging a set of signs above head level.

Gather This Great Idea!

The *Director CD* has a sign for each site and the Early Childhood room. Other *Leader CDs* have sign files too.

Things to Consider

General Concerns

- How can decorations show that Jesus is the focus of our VBS?
- What areas are off-limits? What limitations or concerns do we have?
- What other events will occur during VBS week that may compete for space?
- Do people who oversee building maintenance need to check our plans?

Getting Materials

- Which materials can we use? Where are they stored?
- Can we ask people to loan or donate items?
- How can we let them know what we need?
- How can decorations be affixed to walls and ceilings?

Getting Help

- What kind of help will we need? How many? Who?
- Who takes care of janitorial tasks and daily cleanup?
- When can we meet? When can we begin to set up?
- Should Decorating Committee members attend VBS meetings?

Special Areas & Needs

- Where will registration tables go?
- Will we have a separate area for Early Childhood registration?
- How can we welcome people as soon as they arrive?
- How can we use decorations to communicate about our Mission Project, Closing Program, and follow-up activities?
- Is our facility accessible for attendees with special needs?

Decorating Sources

Check the *2016 VBS Catalog* and vbs.cph.org to find great decorating pieces! Our huge *Barnyard Roundup Decorating Posters, Bible Story Posters, Bible Memory Verse Posters, Barn Siding Backdrop* (interior), *Cornstalks Backdrop, Green Grass Backdrop, Red Barn Siding Backdrop* (exterior), *Red Bandana Print Pennant Banner, Jesus Stand-Up, Cross Stand-Up, Split Rail Fence Post Set, Cowprint Tablecloth, Straw Table Cover, Rusty Barbwire Cord, Tissue Grass Mat, Farm Animal Whirls, and Fadeless Paper Rolls* will give you a great start! Consult the *Decorating Videos*. Use the Decorating To-Do List to track tasks and progress, and use the Decorator Get List to track the items you need. All of these are found on the *Director CD*.

Finding the best decorating items is like going on a giant scavenger hunt! Explore these resources to stretch your budget:

- **Ask congregation members.** Publicize your list of needs ASAP in your church newsletters and bulletins and on your website and bulletin boards, asking people to purchase or lend items.

- **Print Supply Request Tags** found on the *Director CD*. Write items needed on the tags. Hang on a themed bulletin board. Invite people to take a tag, promising to purchase or lend the item(s).

- **Collect donations in boxes** placed in a visible location. Keep your supply lists updated wherever you publish them!

- **Check** garage sales, thrift shops, estate sales, and church storage areas for needed objects.

- **Use the Internet** to find bargains on all kinds of decor and supplies.

- **Ask for donations or loans** from local businesses. Return borrowed items promptly.

- **Connect with other churches** using *Barnyard Roundup* to share ideas or decorating items. Meet other Directors on our Facebook page (ConcordiaVBS) and other social networking sites. Look for links from the Concordia VBS website at vbs.cph.org.

- **Have a decorating party** to make murals and other items.

- **Check catalogs for ideas and resources**, including the *2016 VBS Catalog* and **vbs.cph.org**.

Decorating Common Spaces

Doing VBS with purpose means that your decorations will incorporate crosses, pictures of Jesus, the *Bible Story Posters*, and the *Bible Memory Verse Posters*. Decorate entryways, hallways, doorways, bulletin boards, and other common areas with thematic props: cornstalks, hay bales, fences, barns, sunflowers, and farm decor.

Theme-based backdrops are a key visual! Directions for creating the colorful backdrops you see in our materials are provided on the *Director CD*. You can watch it being painted on the *Decorating Videos* on the *Farm-tastic Overview DVD*.

Common Decor

There are several key pieces of decor that can be used in any area for barnyard decorating that is easy-breezy! 𝒯 = Do-It-Yourself Decorating Project (see *Director CD*)

Backdrops. Decorate with the *Cornstalks Backdrop, Green Grass Backdrop, Barn Siding Backdrop* (interior), and *Red Barn Siding Backdrop* (exterior). See details in the *2016 VBS Catalog*. Or make the 𝒯*Sunrise Backdrop*.

Barnyard Roundup **Decorating Objects.** Use *Jesus Stand-Up* with sheep and the *Cross Stand-Up* to put Jesus front and center. The *Split Rail Fence Post Set*, "hay bales" (boxes wrapped with *Straw Table Covers),* or fences made with *Rusty Barbwire Cord* create your barnyard look.

DIY Decorating Objects have been designed for rotations sites, but the 𝒯Front Porch Stand-Up, 𝒯Windmill, 𝒯Sunflowers with Hay Bales, 𝒯Balloon Pigs, 𝒯Hay Bales, 𝒯Paper Plate Chickens, 𝒯Chicken Coop, 𝒯Sunflower Garden, 𝒯Produce Stand, 𝒯Farm Stand Uprights, 𝒯Old Fashioned Clothesline, and 𝒯Tractor might also be perfect for your common decor. See directions on the *Director CD*.

Farm decor. Use wheelbarrows, old-fashioned water pumps, bushel baskets, galvanized watering cans and buckets, and other farm items to decorate your spaces. Think "safety first" and avoid sharp implements.

Tarps. Canvas and plastic tarps are a VBS staple. Available at home improvement stores, use canvas tarps and green and brown plastic tarps on the floor.

Cardboard grass. Cut spiky grass shapes from cardboard boxes and paint them green and brown to decorate your barnyard.

Colorful **Farm Animal Whirls** and **Red Bandana Print Pennant Banners**. These items give fun pops of color to halls, stairwells, and site locations. Balloons can be fun too!

Gossamer rolls. Available online and in party stores, rolls of gossamer can be used to add a pond to your pasture or can be hung from the ceiling as clouds. After VBS, roll them up and save them for next year!

Huge Decorating Posters
(Included in *Starter Kit*)

The huge *Barnyard Roundup Decorating Posters* make it quicker and easier than ever to add the little details that make a big difference. Long before VBS begins, use the large Theme Poster at your registration site. Add signs with the dates of VBS, sign-up process for students and volunteers, and donation lists for crafts, snacks, and other supplies.

The second poster is filled with farm animals: pigs, a lamb, and a cow! Post them on walls or mount them on cardboard or foam board (add a triangle to the back for an easel). There is also a sign for the Bountiful Blessings Snack Site!

The third poster offers more farm animals and a banner for your registration table. Simply cut out the banner and add it to your registration table. What a quick and easy way to identify and decorate this important first stop for VBS!

Look for the ways figures are used and noted in these Decorating pages, in the pictures throughout the Guide, and on the Decorating Videos on the *Farm-tastic Overview DVD* and at vbs.cph.org.

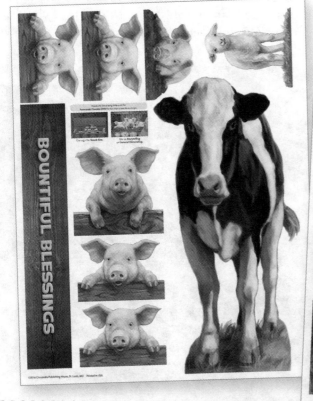

Site Decorating

Each site has a specific purpose and suggestions for an ideal location. You will need to compare this chart with the realities of your VBS space. Adapt as necessary!

Decorate a little or a lot, considering volunteers, time, and budget. Here are some suggested locations and decorations for each site.

Kids	Teams	Main Decor
Opening/Closing	**Church sanctuary or large gathering space**	Front Porch set with ⊤Sunrise Backdrop, ⊤Front Porch Stand-Up, ⊤Windmill, rocking chair, Theme Poster, other farm accessories, *Cross Stand-Up, Split Rail Fence Post Set,* ⊤Sunflowers with Hay Bales, Mission Project poster
Storytelling	Large space— indoors or out	*Bible Story Posters, Barn Siding Backdrop* (interior), *Split Rail Fence Post Set,* ⊤Balloon Pigs, *Barnyard Roundup Decorating Poster* pigs, ⊤Hay Bales, brown tarps, farm finishing touches, stuffed burlap bags, ⊤Paper Plate Chickens, *Red Bandana Print Pennant Banner*
Bible Challenge	Multipurpose room	*Bible Memory Verse Posters,* ⊤Old Fashioned Clothesline, *Cornstalks Backdrop, Green Grass Backdrop,* ⊤Tractor, ⊤Hay Bales, *Straw Table Cover, Split Rail Fence Post Set, Barnyard Roundup Decorating Posters* sheep and lambs (mounted), *Jesus Stand-Up*
Snacks	Outside or multipurpose room	*Bible Story Posters,* ⊤Produce Stand, *Red Barn Siding Backdrop,* ⊤Farm Stand Uprights, from the *Decorating Poster* Bountiful Blessings sign, *Rusty Barbwire Cord*
Games	Outside or gym	⊤Hay Bales, *Red Bandana Print Pennant Banner*
Crafts	Multipurpose room near a sink	*Bible Story Posters, Cowprint Tablecloths,* ⊤Cow Centerpiece, *Tissue Grass Mat, Red Bandana Print Pennant Banner, Farm Animal Whirls*
Registration Table and Photo Op	Entry area	⊤**Registration Table** uses Banner on the *Decorating Poster, Red Barn Siding Backdrop* and *Barn Door Props,* Theme Poster, *Split Rail Fence Post Set,* ⊤Hay Bales, and ⊤Photo Op Set
Halls and Doors	Wherever VBS is happening!	*Farm Animal Whirls* and *Red Bandana Print Pennant Banner* from the ceilings, *Balloons, Barnyard Roundup Decorating Poster animals* on the walls, colorful crepe-paper streamers for doors

⊤ = Do-It-Yourself Decorating Project (see instructions on the *Director CD*)
Consider our *Mounting Tabs* and *Hanging Poles.*

Gather 'Round Opening and Closing— Decorate and Organize!

Oh come, let us worship and bow down; let us kneel before the LORD, *our Maker! Psalm 95:6*

Gather 'Round Opening and Closing is where children begin and end *Barnyard Roundup*. Check out these ideas to set up a fantastic environment for Opening and Closing! Locating this site in the sanctuary will familiarize children with this central place of your parish's life together.

Gather This Great Idea!

If you do the Opening and Closing in the sanctuary of your church, take care to highlight the altar. You want visitors to your church to see this focal point of the church's life together! Move thematic decorations to either side of the altar area.

Opening and Closing Set

Our colorful and super-simple ⚒ **Sunrise Backdrop** can be painted with directions provided on the *Director CD*. See it made in the *Decorating Videos* on the *Farm-tastic Overview DVD* and at vbs.cph.org. Cover the floor with a green tarp.

Make the ⚒ **Front Porch Stand-Up** and the ⚒ **Windmill** using the directions on the *Leader DVD*. Add a rocking chair and a dinner bell for a finishing touch.

Mount the *Decorating Poster* with the kids and the wheelbarrow for your Opening and Closing area.

See the "Decorate!" section on the *Leader DVD* and the *Decorating Videos* on the *Farm-tastic Overview* for specific instructions.

⚒ = Do-It-Yourself Decorating Project (see *Director CD*)

Basics for Opening and Closing

- Provide a focal point in the front for the Opening/Closing Leader with enough room for a screen for the videos and space for the leaders.

- Make sure a cross is the central part of your focal point. The *Cross Stand-Up* in the *2016 VBS Catalog* is a great piece to use.

- Provide a podium for the leader that fits the decor. Be creative!

- Define the seating area. Mark it off with tape, plants, or rugs. If your Opening and Closing area is in a multipurpose room, let children sit on carpet squares, rugs, or mats. If your site is in the church sanctuary, use the pews or chairs for seating.

- A Site Sign for this area is on the *Leader DVD*.

- To store supplies and props, use *VBS Tote Bags* or wicker baskets.

- Add sections of the *Split Rail Fence Post Set* to create a stall. ↑**Sunflowers with Hay Bales** make a great added touch.

Mission Project Decorating Resource

This year's Mission Project is *Tin Roofs for Africa*. Our mission partner is The Lutheran Church—Missouri Synod. See complete details in the project brochure in the *Starter Kit*, the description on page 22, or the *2016 VBS Catalog*. The brochure opens up into a poster you can use to keep track of the offerings for this Mission Project. You can also create a mission area in your Gather 'Round Opening and Closing area. Wouldn't a church with a tin roof be fun?

Use the area as a collection site for your Mission Project offerings. Each time the offerings are collected in the Opening, the leader offers a prayer asking God to bless these offerings and the ministry of *Tin Roofs for Africa*.

↑ = **Do-It-Yourself Decorating Project** (see *Director CD*)

Barn Raising Storytelling— Decorate and Organize!

[Jesus said,] "Blessed rather are those who hear the word of God and keep it!" Luke 11:28

In *Barnyard Roundup* VBS, the kids are actively involved in the telling of the Bible accounts from God's Holy Word. The kids read and see the Bible, God's Holy Word, each lesson. That experience is one you will create with simple, imaginative, easy-to-obtain sets and props. This is where God's life-giving Word is taught!

Basics for Storytelling

- Select a space away from other sites to minimize distractions and noise.
- Provide room for up to 35 people (5 Teams with 6 students and a leader).
- Provide a blank place to hang up all five *Bible Story Posters*. The posters help students visualize the stories. With all five posted, you can review and make connections.
- Place a Storyteller chair near your backdrop. How about a rocking chair?

- Place a large cross that you can hang or put on a stand in front of your storytelling wall. Check out the *Cross Stand-Up* in the *2016 VBS Catalog*!
- Put props near the Storyteller's chair and use *VBS Tote Bags*, baskets, or buckets to store supplies.
- Post a Storytelling Site Sign where the children will enter daily (on the *Director CD*).
- Close the entrance so the interior cannot be seen until the groups enter your area.
- Provide a small table to use for the "Science in the Sheep Pen" experiences.
- Designate floor seating for each Team. Use plastic gingham tablecloths, rugs, or picnic blankets. Provide a few chairs with backs and arms for kids or adults who cannot sit on the floor.
- Use the life-size *Jesus Stand-Up* and make stand-up sheep (instructions on *Leader CD*) from the *Barnyard Roundup Decorating Posters* to show Jesus, our Good Shepherd.

Decorative Objects

Backdrop. Cover your walls with the *Barn Siding Backdrop*, available from the *2016 VBS Catalog*. Hang with the repositionable *Mounting Tabs*. Add sections *Split Rail Fence Post Set* to create a stall. Fill it with ⚐**Balloon Pigs.** Use pink balloons, pink chenille wire, and permanent marker to create these. Add more pigs to the fence posts from the *Barnyard Roundup Decorating Posters*. Mount them on cardboard or foam board. Images also available as clip art on the *Director CD*.

⚐**Hay Bales.** Storytelling uses ⚐**Hay Bales** to create the story sets. Make six from packing boxes wrapped with the *Straw Table Cover*. Cover a cooler with a *Straw Table Cover* and you have a ⚐**Hay Bale** you can sit on! See detailed directions on the *Leader CD*.

Barn floor seating. Spread brown tarps for "barn floor." Borrow them, or purchase them at home improvement stores.

Finishing Touches. There are all kinds of props that can be added in your barn. Buckets, ladders, a wheelbarrow, shovels and rakes, and even a manger help make the set look authentic and interesting. Fill burlap sacks with paper to create "bags of grain" in the barn. Add some ⚐**Paper Plate Chickens** to place around the barn. Hang *Red Bandana Print Pennant Banner* from the ceiling for a pop of color.

See the "Decorate!" section on the *Leader CD* and the *Decorating Videos* on the *Farm-tastic Overview* for specific instructions.

⚐ = Do-It-Yourself Decorating Project (see *Director CD* and *Storytelling Leader CD*)

Gather This Great Idea!

Check out the *Decorating Videos* on the *Farm-tastic Overview DVD* and at vbs.cph.org for ideas for this site!

Green Pastures Bible Challenge—Decorate and Organize!

"But the word of the Lord remains forever." And this word is the good news that was preached to you.
1 Peter 1:25

God's saving Word is the focus of this site. The goals of this site are to learn the Bible Memory Verse through song and to connect that Bible Memory Verse to the Bible story, Take-Home Point, and our lives. The Holy Spirit will have a powerful effect through God's Word on the children in your VBS! These decorating suggestions and tips will help you set the stage for teaching God's Word!

A main feature of the site is an 🔨 **Old Fashioned Clothesline**. Each day at Bible Challenge, the Bible Memory Verse Code Sheets will be clothes pinned to the line by members of the Teams. You can also post them with temporary hooks on a wall or hang a line between two trees if you are outside.

Post the Bible Challenge Site Sign (*Leader CD*) to identify your site.

Gather This Great Idea!

Remember, the first stop for VBS decorating is in your storage closet! At *Barnyard Roundup*, we used backdrops, artificial greenery, cardboard grass, tarps, and pennants—all were great decorations from past VBS years.

Basics for Bible Challenge

Use the *Cornstalks Backdrop* with the *Green Grass Backdrop* for a pasture. Add green tarps on the floor to create "Green Pastures." Show Jesus, our Good Shepherd, with the *Jesus Stand-Up* and make stand-up sheep from the *Barnyard Roundup Decorating Posters*.

Provide room for 35 people (5 Teams with 6 students and a leader) to move around for song actions.

Hang up the five *Bible Memory Verse Posters* around your room and the Bible Challenge Site Sign near the door.

Decorating Elements

Bible Challenge activities provide a fun and creative way to engage children while teaching the Bible Memory Verse. Team groups decipher the Bible Memory Verse Code and then share it by attaching the pieces to the ⸸ **Old Fashioned Clothesline** for everyone to see and read together.

Backdrop. Use the *Cornstalks Backdrop* with the *Green Grass Backdrop* for a pasture. Hang with the repositionable *Mounting Tabs*. Add sections from the *Split Rail Fence Post Set* for your pasture.

⸸ **Tractor.** Create a tractor with two large boxes. Cut windows, make tires out of cardboard, use a pool noodle for a smoke stack, and use disposable cereal bowls for headlights. We made ours blue, but feel free to choose a different color. See detailed directions on the *Leader CD*.

⸸ **Hay Bales.** The Bible Challenge site is jam-packed with exciting activities, so the Green Pastures Leader may want to take a seat on a handy ⸸ **Hay Bale** made out of a large cooler wrapped with a *Straw Table Cover*. Create additional bales for your environment using packing boxes. See detailed directions on the *Leader CD*.

Sheep and lambs. Mount the sheep and lambs from the *Barnyard Roundup Decorating Posters* on cardboard or foam board. Tape on a foam-board triangle for an easel, and place these kid-pleasing animals near the life-size *Jesus Stand-Up*. Images also available as clip art on the *Director CD*.

Check out the *Decorating Videos* on the *Farm-tastic Overview DVD* or at vbs.cph.org.

⸸ = Do-It-Yourself Decorating Project (see *Director CD* and *Bible Challenge Leader CD*)

Seating

The Teams will sit together on the floor. If you want to provide defined spaces for each group, use plastic gingham tablecloths or borrow rugs or blankets of different colors to lay on the floor of your site.

Team Supply Containers

Use *VBS Tote Bags* or mini bushel baskets. Fill with the supplies needed for Teams each day. This will include Bibles and other daily supplies.

Bountiful Blessing Snacks— Decorate and Organize!

The eyes of all look to You, and You give them their food in due season. You open Your hand; You satisfy the desire of every living thing. Psalm 145:15–16

Learning about Jesus while creating with food and eating snacks—kids love it! At Bountiful Blessings Snacks, you use tasty and nourishing food to help the kids remember the Bible stories and Take-Home Points and energize kids for more VBS fun. *Barnyard Roundup* snacks are easy and fun for kids to make. Active kids have active brains, which they will use to learn more about the amazing grace Jesus gives.

It's great when the Snack Site picks up on the theme of the week through its food offerings and decorations. Your local setting will determine where you serve snacks. (Snack Leaders appreciate being near water for easy cleanup.) Set up your area to provide a great environment for making snacks, eating, and sharing God's Word. Check out the *Decorating Videos* on the *Farm-tastic Overview DVD* or at vbs.cph.org for more ideas for VBS decorating.

Basics for Snacks

Set up tables and chairs for 35 people—that's 5 Teams.

Set up an extra table or two for supplies and a demonstration area.

Cover all tables to protect surfaces in keeping with the theme ideas. We used colorful plastic tablecloths with farm decorations. You can also put strips of brown packing or white butcher paper over the tops of the tables. Replace paper as needed.

Create shade if you are outside. Make a focal point for your site by putting your serving table under a canopy.

Hang up a Bountiful Blessings Snacks Sign (*Director CD*) by the entrance to your space.

Option: Have the kids sit on picnic blankets or tarps instead of at tables. Everyone likes a picnic!

Decorative Objects

- **Display the bountiful blessing God gives with a** *𝒯 Produce Stand* for your background. See the detailed directions on the *Leader CD* and check out the *Decorating Videos*.

- **Decorate the walls** with a *Red Barn Siding Backdrop*. Hang with the repositionable *Mounting Tabs*.

- **Frame your snack table with** *𝒯 Farm Stand Uprights.* To make this item, see the detailed directions on the *Leader CD* and check out the *Decorating Videos*. Add the Bountiful Blessings sign from the *Decorating Posters* to the header.

- **Finish off the rest of the tables** in your snack area with colored tablecloths, burlap, sunflowers, or even our *Rusty Barbwire Cord*. Kids will think it's real, but it is actually soft cording!

𝒯 = Do-It-Yourself Decorating Project (see *Director* CD)

Gather This Great Idea!
Check out the *Decorating Videos* on the *Director CD* for ideas for this site!

Udderly Cool Crafts—Decorate and Organize!

Let the favor of the Lord our God be upon us, and establish the work of our hands upon us; yes, establish the work of our hands! Psalm 90:17

At Udderly Cool Crafts, you share God's Word each lesson through engaging and fun crafts that help kids understand and remember the daily Bible stories and Take-Home Points. Craft-making engages hands and hearts so that God's Word sticks. Kids can share crafts with a message as they share God's Word with the world.

Basics for Crafts

- **For a backdrop for the craft area,** use the *Cornstalks Backdrop* with the *Green Grass Backdrop* for a "green pasture." Hang with the *Mounting Tabs*. Add the cow from the *Barnyard Roundup Decorating Posters*. Mount on cardboard or foam board with a triangle piece to make it stand. Add the *Split Rail Fence Post Set*. **Another background option** is to use the *Theme Decorating Poster* (with the kids in the wheelbarrow).

- **Set up tables and chairs** for up to 35 people (5 Teams). Set up an extra table or two for supplies and a demonstration area.

- **Place plastic paint tarps or another protective material** under and around tables to protect the floor from spills.

- **Add plastic *Cowprint Tablecloths* as table coverings.** Place pencils, paintbrushes, crayons, and other supplies in mini bushel baskets, galvanized buckets, or other containers on the tables for easy access. Put strips of packing or butcher paper over the tops of the tables. Replace paper as needed.

- **Make sure there is a cross in your room**—Jesus is God's Son, our Savior and Lord!

- **Hang the Udderly Cool Craft Sign,** from the *Director CD*, at your door.

- **Hang up *Bible Story Posters*** to refer to as you explain the connection between each craft and its Bible story. These are available in the *2016 VBS Catalog*.

Decorative Objects

- **Decorate your tables.** Put a section of a *Tissue Grass Mat* down the center and secure with tape. Make a ⊤ **Cow Centerpiece** to place in the center of the mat with directions provided on the *Director CD*. Add *Red Bandana Print Pennant Banner* around the perimeter. Check out the *Decorating Videos* on the *Farm-tastic Overview DVD* and at vbs.cph.org.

- ⊤ **Cardboard Grass.** Cut the long edge of a flattened cardboard box with grass blade and leaf shapes. Paint the shapes in different shades of greens and browns to create grass for your pasture.

- **Be "udderly cool" and decorate the door.** Tape crepe paper streamers along the top of the doorway. Alternate black and white to be "udderly cool." Make the streamers about five feet long—no tripping!

- *Farm Animal Whirls.* Put these outside your door, around the edge of the demonstration tables, and in other places for pops of color.

⊤ = Do-It-Yourself Decorating Project (see *Director* CD)

Gather This Great Idea!

Check out the *Decorating Videos* on the *Farm-tastic Overview DVD* for more ideas!

6. Recruit, Train, Retain!

To have an effective VBS program, you need a team of volunteers with energy, creativity, and a commitment to share the Gospel of Jesus Christ with God's children. VBS requires enough volunteers to make children feel secure. You will need the following types of volunteers: Site Leaders and Site Teams, Team Leaders, Support Teams, and Early Childhood Leaders and helpers.

Site Leaders

Site Leaders are the backbone of your VBS. Look for people who share your goals for VBS, enjoy sharing their interests and skills with children, have good organizational skills, and work well with others. Recruiting Site Leaders is a "do-it-first" key task of VBS. Check with the volunteers who served last year. Many VBS folks find a place they love in VBS and want to serve again. When you have key Site Leaders in place, let others know who is providing that leadership as you recruit.

Opening and Closing. Recruit someone with the energy and confidence to lead large groups at the Opening and Closing. Your Pastor would be a good choice. People who volunteer in Sunday School often have these skills. The Opening and Closing Team will need people to lead music, highlight the Mission Project, and take care of any audiovisual needs.

Storytelling and Bible Challenge Leaders. Enlist your best teachers for Storytelling and Bible Challenge. The Storyteller needs an affinity for drama; the Bible Challenge Leader leads hands-on and musical activities.

Craft Leader. Recruit a Craft Leader who has interest and aptitude in craft-making.

Game Leader. Find a Game Leader with the energy and skills to teach games.

Snack Leader. Draft a person who has the gift of hospitality for the Snack Site.

Site Teams to support Site Leaders. Site Leaders need helpers who are willing to assist them. Ask your Site Leaders about who might serve with them; they might be glad to recruit their own teams!

Team Leaders

Team Leaders will be assigned six children to lead to the rotation sites. See the job description on the *Director CD* for additional information. Look for people who like to work with children and who

- are leaders and encouragers, not bosses;
- develop friendships with every child in his or her group;

are witnesses to Jesus Christ through their words and actions as they help and encourage kids to participate, cooperate, and ask questions in order to discover Bible answers;

keep kids focused on tasks and challenges; and

participate in activities with their Team members.

Support Teams

There are lots of VBS tasks that support the program without direct involvement with children. Consider who prefers behind-the-scenes type of work and get them involved in one of the following roles.

Registration Leader. This person leads registration efforts before and during VBS with a team. Our convenient online tool at cph.org/vbsmate makes registration easy! In addition to registration, the tools allow you to assign children to Elementary and Early Childhood Teams and assign Team Leaders. During VBS, this team might include volunteers who meet and greet all VBS kids, with a special focus on nonmembers. On the first days of VBS, it is helpful to have one team member manning registration and check-in for every 40 children expected.

Decoration Leader. With a team, this leader plans the decorations for VBS. Together, they play an important part in the VBS setup, teardown, and cleanup efforts. Recruit setup and teardown crews for extra help.

Publicity Leader. This person leads a team to develop and execute plans to publicize VBS. The plan includes efforts to register children of the congregation, their friends, and kids in the community.

Administration and Support Leader. Working with a team, this leader will assist and support the Director. Tasks may include purchasing and organizing supplies, running errands, and copying and preparing handouts and other printed materials. During VBS, this team can serve as runners and floaters.

Volunteer Recruitment Team. This team supports the volunteer recruitment efforts, staffs the VBS table to explain student registration and volunteer recruitment, and makes phone calls and personal contacts. This team can also help with volunteer training events.

Media Team: This team arranges for media needs at Opening and Closing, takes photographs during VBS, and provides other media services.

Early Childhood Leaders and Helpers

Look for Early Childhood volunteers who are loving, patient, and caring, and who have a strong desire to share Jesus with young children.

Make sure you have enough volunteers to share tasks and responsibilities. This will vary by your location and the size of your Early Childhood registration.

A small program of twenty preschoolers or fewer may need one or two Early Childhood Leaders who handle all the activities with the support of helpers.

Larger programs may recruit Site Leaders similar to the Elementary rotation and group the children in Teams with assigned Team Leaders.

Seven Steps to Recruiting Success

There are many different tasks and types of workers needed to pull off a successful VBS. There are many ways to recruit volunteers. For maximum effectiveness, use a variety of approaches. Start with a strategy you are comfortable with, and consult these "Seven Steps to Recruiting Success."

Step 1: Pray.

- Ask God to help you find leaders to teach and share God's Word.
- Ask church members to pray concerning your recruitment efforts. Provide a piece like the Prayer Calendar on the *Director CD* to provide specific direction for their prayers.
- Ask your Pastor to include prayers for recruitment in your worship time.

Step 2: Determine number of volunteers needed.

- Base staff needs on enrollment numbers from the past two years.
- For Early Childhood, you need about one leader with a helper for every five preschoolers as well as leaders for the sites.
- You need one Team Leader for every six elementary kids.
- You need six Site Leaders. Add Site Helpers as needed.
- Determine Administration and Support Team needs in the areas of Volunteer Recruitment, Registration, Decorations, Setup and Teardown Crews, Publicity, Administration, Audiovisual, and any others.
- Arrange to have one helper for every forty children on the first day for registration and check-in.
- Assemble a Volunteer Recruitment Team.

Step 3: Identify volunteers.

- Divide tasks among the Recruitment Team.
- Seek active, committed Christians from all stages of life who enjoy children.
- Ask your Pastor, church staff, and church leaders to suggest volunteer names.
- List possible volunteers on the Volunteer Recruitment Log on the *Director CD*. Use job descriptions to guide your search; find these on the *Director CD*.
- Seek people with flexible work schedules or who get time off for service projects.

- Check your church's child-safety policies. See more info in the "Safety" section.
- Allow enough time to process background checks before the beginning of VBS.

Step 4: Recruit volunteers.

- Set a positive tone and show enthusiasm and love for your VBS.
- Use the chart of Volunteer Recruitment Strategies on the *Director CD* to guide you.
- Invite volunteering through worship bulletins, parish newsletters, and a themed registration table.
- Show recruitment commercials from the *Farm-tastic Overview DVD* in the *Starter Kit* before or after worship services and at church meetings.
- Use phone, email, Facebook, or a letter asking individuals to volunteer.
- Send a mailing to your list of possible volunteers with a Volunteer Recruitment Letter (*Director CD*) and a job description for a position that fits what you know of them. A short hand-written sentence on the letter personalizes this mailing and truly makes a positive difference in the volunteer's response! When volunteers know what you are asking them to do and the positive impact they will make, and when they have a chance to think and pray about it, the answer is more often yes.
- Distinguish appeals for positions based on skill and preparation levels required.
- Hang the Volunteer Sign-Up Sheet (*Director CD*) in high-traffic areas of your church.
- Make personal contact to fill skilled positions, such as musicians, sound technicians, and Site Leaders.
- Give time for a response. Ask people to help; then give them time to pray, think, and check their schedules. Request an answer by a designated time, perhaps a week, and then check back for a response.
- When volunteers say yes, provide them with the information and materials they need to accomplish the role.
- If volunteers say no, honor their decision and avoid making them feel uncomfortable. If a candidate declines to serve, see if you can find out why. Keep the door open for future service.
- Accept part-time help, but seek consistency for Team and Site Leader volunteers.

- Provide copies of your final Team Chart for your leaders, Pastor, and church staff (*Director CD*).
- Call, call, call and talk, talk, talk. A telephone call works! Even better is a face-to-face conversation. Start with volunteers from previous years to begin filling your spots. Ask a couple of volunteers to help with your call campaign. Provide a script if needed.

Step 5: Provide training and resources for volunteers.

- Give volunteers their resources and supplies early so they can prepare.
- Provide a training event for volunteers. Use the outline provided in the "Volunteer Training" section.
- Hand out the Every Leader Pack. (See specifics in "Volunteer Training.")
- Share your child-safety policies at the training sessions.

Step 6: Care for your volunteers.

- Provide training and resources. Let volunteers know you will help; then support them.
- Pair experienced volunteers with less-experienced ones to build confidence.
- Provide tips and support for working with kids with special needs.
- Provide tips for effective discipline.
- Affirm, thank, and recognize volunteers.
- Provide childcare for volunteers who have infants and toddlers.

Step 7: Support, nurture, and thank volunteers.

- Use the Volunteer Commissioning on the *Director CD* in a worship service right before VBS. See the *Pastor's Overview* for more information.
- Acknowledge volunteers, and encourage the church to show its support.
- Purchase T-shirts to identify volunteers. See our T-shirts in the *VBS 2016 Catalog* and vbs.cph.org.
- Make a nametag for each volunteer.
- Connect with every volunteer at least once a day.
- Pray together each day before children arrive.
- Create a "volunteer lounge" with snacks, drinks, supplies, and posted announcements.
- Schedule breaks for all volunteers.
- Let Site Leaders rest during one rotation, if you can.
- Ask Site Teams to meet briefly after VBS to plan and pray for the next day.
- Express appreciation for your volunteers in formal and informal ways. Check out ideas in the "Daily encouragements and thank yous" section.

- *VBS Tote Bags* from CPH (sample found in *Starter Kit*) make an excellent appreciation gift. Check the catalog for more details.

Ways to thank your volunteers

- Verbally thank volunteers in large gatherings, at the daily closings, in the Closing Program, and in the worship service immediately following VBS.
- If your church features VBS on its website or shares photo albums or other media, acknowledge the dedicated service of the VBS staff there too!
- Give each volunteer a Thank-You Certificate. You'll find one on the *Director CD*.
- Thank each volunteer by name in bulletins and in the next church newsletter.
- Host a thank-you lunch to celebrate the efforts of all volunteers following VBS. Ask them to share stories.
- Communicate the impact of VBS and the service of the volunteers in a follow-up thank-you letter. Share statistics on enrollment and Mission Project results. Let volunteers know about plans to follow up with nonmember VBS families.

Daily encouragements and thank yous

Encourage volunteers with daily notes and small gifts. Personalize notes with clip art from the *Director CD*. Add invitations to a volunteer appreciation event.

Consider using these ideas in your staff room, or distribute them to each person.

Lesson 1: For "Jesus Cares," paint wooden sheep shapes. Attach a note that says, "Thank you for caring for Jesus' lambs at *Barnyard Roundup*!" Include John 10:14–15.

Lesson 2: For "Jesus Provides," provide a loaf of bread or "bread in a jar." Attach a note like this one: "Jesus provides our daily bread for our body and food for our souls in God's Word! P.S. Thank you for sharing God's Word with the kids!"

Lesson 3: For "Jesus Leads," provide a pack of sunflower seeds. Use our Sunflower Decor shape for this note: "Thanks for sowing the seed of God's Word at VBS today! God will provide an abundant harvest!"

Lesson 4: For "Jesus Forgives," provide a snack bag of chocolates with the note, "Sweetest news ever: Jesus forgives! Thanks for sharing this sweet message at VBS!"

Lesson 5: For "Jesus is our Savior," fill a treat bag with candy hearts. Attach this note: "Thanks for sharing the love of Jesus, our Savior, with our kids at *Barnyard Roundup*!"

Thank-you gifts for any theme

Give volunteers a daisy-type flower with a note: "God

loves you. We love you. That's the truth!"

Give volunteers a bag of pretzels with this note: "Pretzels remind us of arms folded in prayer. We are praying for you today as you serve God's beloved children!"

Attach this note to a water: "Thanks for keeping cool and sharing the refreshing Good News that Jesus loves us!"

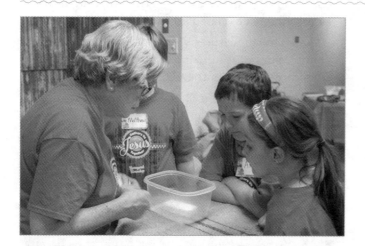

Volunteer Training

Training benefits your volunteers. Well-prepared volunteers lead with confidence. They excel with clear expectations and plans. They have fewer discipline problems. Children blossom in such an environment. In short, everyone benefits!

Make training a team effort. As VBS Director, you are responsible for volunteer training, but you don't have to lead it all yourself. Ask your Pastor, Director of Christian Education, teachers, or other qualified persons to help. Check the Concordia VBS site (vbs. cph.org) to find out about workshops in your area.

Get VBS materials to Site Leaders. As you recruit your Site Leaders, provide them with their Leader Guide and other materials as soon as you can. This gives them plenty of time to prepare, especially if they are helping with the Volunteer Training.

Plan training for Team Leaders. Decide if you will involve Team Leaders (who lead the Teams of children around the sites) in training with the Site Leaders or if you will train them separately, as described at the end of the Training Agenda. Team Leaders will do better with these tasks if you show them how and let them practice. Team Leaders lead discussions at the Storytelling Site. They also lead their small group in an activity at the Bible Challenge Site. They discuss "Game Points" at Games.

Decide when and how long. VBS Directors report they schedule two to four hours of volunteer training. Some have several meetings; others have one longer session. Most offer sessions at different times so people can attend at the time that works best for them. Schedule your first training four to eight weeks before VBS; finish no fewer than ten days ahead to allow sufficient planning time.

Customize this outline. Use the training outline on the next pages to lead a 3-hour-and-45-minute session. Take more time on each section, if you have time. Pick and choose, if you have less. More materials for training are found in the "Training" section on the *Director CD*.

VBS Training Agenda

3 hours and 45 minutes (Make this fit your time frame.)

Step 1: Welcome and Opening Devotion (20 minutes)

Step 2: Gather for *Barnyard Roundup* (30 minutes)

Break (10 minutes)

Step 3: Bible study (50 minutes)

Break (10 minutes)

Step 4: Your Program's Basic Data and Important Dates (30 minutes)

Step 5: Rotate to Three Sites (30 minutes)

Break (5 minutes)

Step 6: Q & A and Get Acquainted (30 minutes)

Step 7: Large-Group Closing Prayer (10 minutes)

Training Preparation

- Set the date(s) and time(s) for training.
- Get drinks, food, and supplies.
- Arrange for childcare.
- Invite your Pastor to be the Bible study leader. If he is unable, ask for his recommendation.
- Give your Bible study leader a copy of the Lesson Summary (page 4) and Step 3 instructions (page 57) at least a week early.
- Recruit three people to lead Games, Snacks, and Music rotation sites for three 10-minute sessions in Step 5 (pp. 58–60). Ask these leaders for their help. Give each a copy of the instructions from Step 5. Be sure to arrange for supplies for these activities. Review the training outline and resources thoroughly.
- Plan your Every Leader Pack of handouts. Copy and assemble pages from the *Director Guide, Director CD,* and your local handouts. See the list of suggested handouts on page 54.
- Fill out the Team Chart from the *Director CD* so it can be distributed to all. With permission, add phone numbers and email addresses so volunteers can contact one another.
- Prepare local handout material. This will include a daily schedule for the rotations, as well as the locations of the various sites. There may be a VBS calendar with dates for the Closing Program and other important activities, such as volunteer commissioning, an appreciation lunch, and worship services before and after *Barnyard Roundup.* You may wish to distribute written expectations for the volunteers, including job descriptions.
- Get staff identity items ready to hand out (e.g., *Barn-dana Team Identifiers* or T-shirts).
- Prepare your local handouts for first-aid procedures and emergency plans, child-safety policies, and discipline guidelines.
- Prepare nametags.
- Plan refreshments, such as a drink and simple snacks, that will be available as your volunteers arrive.

Setup on Training Day

- Set up a television and a DVD player to show the *Farm-tastic Overview DVD* and *Song-Action DVD.*
- Set up equipment to show PowerPoint presentations from the *Director CD* that correlate to the training script.
- Find the PowerPoint resources in the "Training" section of the *Director CD.*
- Set up a CD player to play the audio *Music CD* (*Music Leader Guide*).
- Place Every Leader Packs, supplies, and handouts on a table. Ask volunteers to pick up handout materials as they arrive.
- Set up sites for Games, Snacks, and Music; see Step 5 (p. 58).
- Set Bibles and pencils on tables.
- Set out drinks and food items.

Resources Needed for Training Session

- Farm-tastic Overview DVD
- Early Childhood and Elementary Leaflets
- Good Times Music Leader Guide's 2-Disc Set (Music CD and Song-Action DVD)
- Television/projection system for Farm-tastic Overview DVD
- Director CD
- Polly the Pig Puppet
- Confirm commitments with the Bible study leader and three training rotation leaders (Snacks, Crafts, and Music). Materials are listed in "Training Preparation."

- Game supplies for the "Gather the Eggs" game. (See p. 59.)
- Snack supplies for the "Follow the Flock" snack. (See p. 60.)
- Every Leader Packets copied and assembled. (See below.)
- Drinks and snacks (provided in addition to the Snack that is part of the training)
- Nametags
- Pencils or pens
- Bell or triangle to use as a signal
- Bibles

Every Leader Packet Handouts

Assemble an Every Leader Packet with copies of each of the items below. Team Leaders Pages are copied just for those volunteers, as they will not be needed by volunteers running the rotation sites.

Copy from this Guide

- Page 3: Welcome page
- Page 4: Barnyard Roundup Lesson Summary
- Page 5: Session Schedule

Copy from the Director CD

- Farm-tastic Bingo Sheet
- Purpose & Goals Worksheet, filled out
- Team Chart, filled out. Add phone numbers and email addresses, if you have permission to share them.

- Leader Devotions and Share the Gospel Sheet

Copies of your local schedules and expectations

- Your daily schedule, locations of sites, current enrollment data, and any other local information
- Volunteer Commissioning, Closing Program, and special events details
- First-aid procedures and emergency plans
- Child-safety policies
- Discipline guidelines

Copies for the Team Leaders only

- Team Leader Pages, one for each Team Leader, plus a few extras

Barnyard Roundup Training Agenda

Step 1: Welcome and Opening Devotion (20 minutes)

As volunteers arrive, warmly welcome them and introduce yourself. You may ask them to sign in with their name and their role at this year's VBS. Give them the chart of the week's activities and other materials for the session and ask them to find a seat. Load Training PowerPoint.

(Slide 1) **SAY:** Welcome to our training for this year's VBS, *Barnyard Roundup: Jesus gathers us together.*

From the Every Leader Packet, have the group read the "Welcome to *Barnyard Roundup!*" page. Ask the volunteers to note at the bottom of this page the ways to be in touch with Concordia Publishing House and with other VBS leaders through Facebook, the CPH VBS website, and email. Also note the feedback survey information; Concordia Publishing House wants to hear from you!

SAY: In *Barnyard Roundup* VBS, our children learn that Jesus gathers us together! Kids want to belong, be understood, and be valued. They want a BFF by their side, no matter what! At *Barnyard Roundup*, kids will discover that Jesus is better than a BFF. Jesus, their Savior, knows them by name, rounds them up, and brings them home. He is with us always and forever, no matter what!

(Slide 2) **SAY:** Psalm 23 is the Bible Memory focus. This beloved Psalm shares our confident trust that our Lord is with us now and forever.

Everything we do this week is designed to share God's Word and His amazing plan with the children. Because of God's great love for us all, Jesus, our Good Shepherd, came to earth to lay down His life for us to pay for our sins and give us eternal life. Jesus loves us and gives us victory over our sin, death, and the devil through His death and resurrection. Jesus, our Savior, gathers us together now and forever.

(Slide 3) You may lead the prayer yourself OR pray this prayer together as a group. **SAY:** As we jump into this farm-tastic experience, let's begin with prayer:

Dear Jesus, You are our Good Shepherd. Thank You. You take good care of us and provide everything we need. You save us through Your death and resurrection. Lead us and forgive us. As we serve You and Your children in *Barnyard Roundup*, Jesus, gather us together. Work through us to share Your saving love with them so we will be with you, now and forever. In Your name we pray. Amen.

SAY: Since we're all gathered together, let's get to know one another better and play "Farm-tastic Bingo." (Have group turn to Farm-tastic Bingo Sheets.) Take your Bingo Sheet and a pencil or pen. You'll have seven and a half minutes to connect with the other volunteers and complete as many squares as you can. Learn their name, share yours, and get their signature on a square that matches them. A person can sign only one square on your sheet.

If you complete a bingo, five across any way, yell, "BINGO! FARM-TASTIC!" Everyone will freeze, and you'll quickly introduce the five people in your bingo group, telling everyone a little about them. If we have more time, we'll keep going! Any questions? Seven and a half minutes. GO!

At the conclusion of seven and a half minutes (or whatever time you decide), call STOP. Ask the group to take their seats.

(Slide 4: Barnyard Roundup Lesson Summary) **SAY:** Now that we know one another a little better, let's get to know VBS. Turn to the *Barnyard Roundup* Lesson Summary. In *Barnyard Roundup* VBS, the children learn that Jesus gathers us together! God's Word in the Bible is the center of our VBS, so our kids remember and retain God's Holy Word. Each Lesson has a *My Shepherd Collectible* that depicts the Bible story; a Bible Memory Verse, which is learned in Bible Challenge; and a Take-Home Point, which is repeated throughout the time at the various sites.

SAY: We'll go more in-depth later, but let's get the big picture as we read through each day. Then, starting with Lesson 1, identify the lesson's *My Shepherd Collectible*, the Bible story and its reference, the Take-Home Point, and the Bible Memory Verse.

Then point to the Take-Home Point column and **SAY:** Every leader, every lesson, says and teaches the five Take-Home Points. To help remember the Take-Home Point, you, the leader, will point up and circle your hand twice and say, "GATHER 'ROUND!" Then point up and say the lesson's Take-Home Point, "JESUS CARES!" The Teams join you, and all of you point up and repeat, "JESUS CARES!" Everyone then makes a circle with their hand as they say, "NOW AND FOREVER!" The "Jesus" part changes for each lesson, but the actions remain the same!

(*Slides 5–9*) **SAY: Let's practice all five Take-Home Points! I'll be the leader; you be the kids!** Then lead the group to say the Take-Home Point Call and Response.

LEADER: **GATHER 'ROUND!** (Point up and circle hand.) **JESUS CARES!** TEAMS: (Point up.) **JESUS CARES,** (Circle hand.) **NOW AND FOREVER!**

LEADER: **GATHER 'ROUND!** (Point up and circle hand.) **JESUS PROVIDES!** TEAMS: (Point up.) **JESUS PROVIDES,** (Circle hand.) **NOW AND FOREVER!**

LEADER: **GATHER 'ROUND!** (Point up and circle hand.) **JESUS LEADS!** TEAMS: (Point up.) **JESUS LEADS,** (Circle hand.) **NOW AND FOREVER!**

LEADER: **GATHER 'ROUND!** (Point up and circle hand.) **JESUS FORGIVES!** TEAMS: (Point up.) **JESUS FORGIVES,** (Circle hand.) **NOW AND FOREVER!**

LEADER: **GATHER 'ROUND!** (Point up and circle hand.) **JESUS IS OUR SAVIOR!** TEAMS: (Point up.) **JESUS IS OUR SAVIOR,** (Circle hand.) **NOW AND FOREVER!**

(*Slide 10: Share the Gospel*) **SAY: Check out the Share the Gospel Sheet. You may have noticed that the Take-Home Points do share the Gospel! In fact, the entire point of *Barnyard Roundup* VBS is telling others the Good News that Jesus is our Good Shepherd and Savior from sin who gathers us together in His family and gives us eternal life. Use the expanded Take-Home Points conversation to share God's love in Jesus with our VBS kids. That's not all! There are also two additional methods listed.**

(*Slide 11: Theme Videos*) Using the *Opening/Closing DVD*, show the Lesson 1 *Opening Theme Video*. **SAY: Our elementary students will meet Mark and Jessi in the *Theme Videos* at Opening and Closing each day. These kids have different views about life on their farm! With Jake, their father, both of them learn that Jesus loves them, forgives them, and gathers us all together in His family. As our kids see the videos, they will see how our Take-Home Points connect to our lives right now.**

Step 2: Jumping into *Barnyard Roundup* (30 minutes)

(*Slide 12*) Show the *Program Overview* from the *Farm-tastic Overview DVD*. Afterward, answer any questions about the program. Then have the leaders look at the page "Session Schedule." **SAY: Let's review how our time together goes. The children start the time at the Gather 'Round Opening, where they meet their Team Leaders and the other children in their Team, or small group. If you are a Team Leader, it is important that you greet the parents and have them sign their children in each day. The opening large-group gathering is an important event, as it sets the tone and introduces the theme and Bible story for the day. The children take cues from their Team Leader, who will accompany and guide them from site to site and talk with them about what they are learning and doing.**

(*Slide 13*) **SAY: Now I'd like to introduce the Site Leaders and their helpers.**

Site Leaders, when I introduce you, please tell us who is on your team! Introduce the following:

- Opening/Closing Leader
- Storytelling Leader
- Bible Challenge Leader
- Snack Leader
- Game Leader
- Craft Leader

Thanks, everyone! Each day, after the Opening, the children will rotate among these five rotation sites: Storytelling, Bible Challenge, Crafts, Snacks, and Games.

The Storytelling Site uses drama and action to explore the Bible story. The Team Leaders will use the *Farm Fresh Fun Elementary Leaflets* to talk about "Science in the Sheep Pen" activities and lead discussions about the Bible account.

The Bible Challenge Site focuses on Psalm 23. The children will learn about sheep and shepherds, and sing to help them learn Psalm 23.

At the Games Site, the children play theme-related games. At the Snack Site, children make and eat a theme-related snack. The Craft Site has children making theme-related crafts.

Put the *Polly the Pig Puppet* on your hand. **SAY: This puppet, Polly the Pig, meets early childhood students in the Early Childhood Opening and Closing each day. She's new to the farm and has all sorts of adventures! She will introduce the Bible story and wrap it up each lesson.** Share other information about Early Childhood VBS, including the *Little Sprouts Early Childhood Leaflets*.

SAY: After visiting all the sites, the children return to the Closing to sing, pray, watch a skit, and learn about our Mission Project. Just before going home, we hand out the *My Shepherd Collectibles* with the Bible Memory Verse for the day!

10-Minute Break

Step 3: Bible Study (50 minutes)

Make sure everyone has a Bible and turns to the five Leader Devotions in the Every Leader Pack.

SAY: The most important part of our VBS is the Bible stories. We're going to take the next 50 minutes to get into God's Word, using the Leader Devotions with a few discussion questions.

As time permits, read one or more of the Scriptures aloud and discuss the questions below.

(*Slide 14 Bible Study Questions*) As an option, divide into small groups and post the Bible study questions for all to see. Assign a Bible story to each group to read and discuss. After about 10 minutes, bring everyone back together. Ask each small group to tell about their Scripture, using the Leader Devotions and questions as a guide. **SAY: Here are our Bible study questions:**

1. **What questions do you have about the story?**
2. **How does the Bible story point to Jesus as our Savior from sin?**
3. **How does the Bible story show me how God loves and saves me, now and forever?**

Stop the discussion after 40 minutes. **SAY: We've had some great discussions! Did you notice how each Bible story demonstrates the Take-Home Point of the lesson? I want to encourage you to continue to study these Bible stories on your own or with co-workers, because each one has so much to tell us about Jesus Christ, God's Son, our Savior and our Lord. Let's take a break!**

10-Minute Break

Step 4: Your Program's Basic Data and Important Dates (30 minutes)

(Slide 15) **SAY:** Now it's time to get down to basics for our week of VBS! Let's take the next 30 minutes or so to go over some basic details. Ask the leaders to turn to those pages in the Every Leader Packet. Explain your local details as you cover the following items:

- Schedules
- Expectations
- Closing events and other special events
- First-aid procedures
- Emergency plans
- Child-safety policies
- Discipline guidelines

SAY: This week of VBS will go quickly! We'll need to communicate and keep one another informed. We'll get tired and, at times, frustrated, but let's keep a friendly, positive attitude with the children. I am here to serve you and help you accomplish your VBS job. Does anyone have any questions?

Step 5: Rotate to Three Sites (30 minutes)

(Slide 16) **SAY:** Now we're going to experience parts of *Barnyard Roundup* as the kids will at VBS. Would the three preselected Site Leaders head to your sites? The rest of us will divide into three groups.

Each group is a Team. Choose someone in your group to be your Team Leader. At VBS, Team Leaders take their Teams from site to site. They participate in activities with their kids, and sometimes they lead activities under the direction of a Site Leader.

Now that you are in three Teams, I'm going to send each Team to a site, either Games, Snacks, or Music. When I signal, you will move to the next site. When your Team has visited all three sites, return to your seats.

Music Site: *Good Times* (10 minutes)

You'll need the *Good Times Music Leader Guide (with 2-Disc Set)* from the *Starter Kit*.

On training day, set up multimedia equipment to play the *Song-Action Videos* on the *Song-Action DVD*. Plan to teach several of the songs.

SAY: Welcome to the Music Site! While we don't have a Music Site, we use VBS music in the Opening and Closing and at our Bible Challenge Site.

Let's learn some of our VBS music and some of the actions that go with the songs. We all need to learn the theme song, "Always and Forever, No Matter What!"

5-Minute Break

Game Site: Bales of Fun Games (10 minutes)

Gather the Eggs

Lesson 5

I shall dwell in the house of the LORD forever.
Psalm 23:6

Supply List

4 dozen plastic eggs
(1 dozen of the same color per Team)

4 empty egg cartons

4 farmer hats

Get Ready

In a large playing area, scatter and/or hide all the eggs.

For younger kids, put a color marking on each of the cartons so they remember what color eggs they are looking for. Another adaption for younger players is to scatter the eggs instead of hiding them.

Here We Go

SAY: Well, farmers, it's our last time at Bales of Fun Games! We've had a great time learning all the different ways Jesus gathers us together each and every day. Today, we are talking about a beautiful Bible story where Jesus, right after He rose from the grave, calls Mary by name and calls her as His own. We are all His own, and He gathers us to Himself.

LEADER: GATHER 'ROUND! (Point up and circle hand.) JESUS IS OUR SAVIOR! **TEAMS:** (Point up.) JESUS IS OUR SAVIOR, (Circle hand.) NOW AND FOREVER!

SAY: Just as Jesus gathers us all together, we need to gather the eggs that have been laid all over the place. Before we start the game, each Team needs to pick one person to be the farmer. Your Team also needs to decide one farm animal to be. Make sure the other Teams don't hear what your animal is.

Designate each Team with one color egg and give an egg carton and hat to each farmer.

SAY: When I say, "Go!" all the animals are loose to find their color eggs. However, animals can't pick up eggs, only the farmer can. Also, animals can't talk. They can only make their respective animal noise. The farmers must listen carefully to find their animals, who are hopefully finding all twelve of their eggs. Once the farmer has all twelve eggs in his or her carton, yell "Gather 'round, the eggs are found!" The first Team to find all dozen eggs of their color wins.

You will probably want to play this game again. Quickly scatter the eggs in the playing area and pick a new farmer. If you'd like the added confusion, have the Teams pick a new animal to represent. You could also challenge the Teams to make no noise but only actions to notify their farmer. When finished, have the students sit together with their Team and discuss the Game Points.

Game Points

Team Leaders **ASK:** How are we gathered into the family of God? (Through our Baptism) God calls each and every one of us to be His son or His daughter. As children of God, what good gifts do we receive? (God's love, forgiveness, eternal life) Thanks to Jesus' saving act of the cross, He gives us His love eternal. What awesome news!

LEADER: GATHER 'ROUND! (Point up and circle hand.) JESUS IS OUR SAVIOR! **TEAMS:** (Point up.) JESUS IS OUR SAVIOR, (Circle hand.) NOW AND FOREVER!

Games

Snack Site: Bountiful Blessings Snacks (10 minutes)

Follow the Flock

Lesson 1

Barnyard Roundup
Jesus Gathers Us Together

Supply List

At each Team's table, you will need these things:

- A plate, plastic knife, and toothpick for each child
- 7 small cauliflower florets for each child
- 2 black olives for each child
- Assorted vegetables to serve on the side, such as carrot sticks, cucumber slices, cherry tomatoes, and bell pepper slices
- Ranch dressing or veggie dip
- A small cup or muffin wrapper with dip for each child
- Hand sanitizer, napkins, cups, and water

Advance Preparation

Clean and dry the vegetables. Cut cauliflower into small florets. Each child needs seven florets. Cut and prepare other vegetables, such as carrot sticks and cucumber slices, if desired. Before the session, put items listed in the Supply List on each Team's table.

When Kids Arrive

Gather the kids in your central meeting spot.

SAY: Welcome! At Bountiful Blessings Snacks, we'll learn how Jesus cares for us and gathers us together. Let's make a snack to help us remember Jesus cares. Share the Take-Home Point. **SAY: GATHER 'ROUND!** (Point up and circle hand.) **JESUS CARES!** Teams: (Point up.) **JESUS CARES,** (Circle hand.) **NOW AND FOREVER!**

SAY: Let's say the Bible verse: *"The LORD is my shepherd; I shall not want."* Psalm 23:3. Sheep follow their shepherd. Did you know sheep are gregarious? That's a big word. Say it with me: gregarious. That means sheep stick together. They are born with strong instincts to stay in a large group—a flock—and follow one another. Sticking together helps protect sheep from predators. Their gregarious instinct helps a shepherd to care for them! Sheep want to follow a friendly person who will protect them and lead them

to food and water. Jesus, our Good Shepherd, takes care of us and protects us from sin and the devil. Jesus cares, now and forever!

Making the Snack

SAY: To help you remember this, we're making a snack that looks like a sheep. Demonstrate as you explain: **Arrange the cauliflower. Put the florets in an oval shape in the middle of your plate for the sheep's body. Place a black olive on the left side to be the sheep's face. Use the knife to cut a second black olive into one small piece for an ear and four long pieces for legs. Arrange them on your sheep. Dip a toothpick into the dressing and draw an eye on your sheep's face. Make a pasture by putting green vegetables around the plate. Add flowers to the pasture by cutting tomatoes or red peppers.** Hold up the finished example.

SAY: After you make your edible sheep artwork, dip your veggies in the dressing and enjoy. Help yourself to extra veggies! Jesus, our Shepherd, cares for us by providing this healthy food. Let's thank God for this healthy snack. Lead a snack prayer. Remind kids to clean their hands with sanitizer. Send them to the Team tables to make snacks.

Before They Go

SAY: GATHER 'ROUND! (Point up and circle hand.) **JESUS CARES!** Teams: (Point up.) **JESUS CARES,** (Circle hand.) **NOW AND FOREVER! SAY:** You learned more about gregarious sheep. And you'll learn more about Jesus, our Good Shepherd.

Snacks

Step 6: Q & A and Get Acquainted (30 minutes)

(*Slide 17*) Give time for various VBS volunteer groups to gather to review their plans and ask questions. Ask Site Leaders to meet with Site Helpers. Have Team Leaders meet with you. If you haven't already done so, hand out leader resources. Encourage groups to schedule a time to meet to plan, practice, or decorate. Exchange phone numbers and email addresses.

Step 7: Large-Group Closing Prayer (10 minutes)

(*Slide 18*) **ASK: What makes you most excited about *Barnyard Roundup*? What concerns should we pray about together?** Close with a prayer that incorporates these joys and concerns. Ask God to bless your VBS and your volunteers as preparations continue.

Team Leader Training

(If separate from step-by-step training on pages 55–61)

Team Leaders have direct contact with kids every lesson and benefit from training for these challenges. Involve them in step-by-step training, or schedule their own event. If possible, offer Team Leader training at several different times and places. Extend the training schedule time in order to study all five Bible stories. Team Leaders will do a better job if they know the stories well. Finish training a week before your VBS starts.

Team Leader Pages

Use the Team Leader Pages located on the *Director CD* as an outline for Team Leader training. Make sure all Team Leaders have a copy of their Team Leader Pages with the *Barnyard Roundup* Lesson Summary (p. 4). These pages give leadership helps and directions for the activities they lead each day. Print them from the *Director CD*. Set a positive, joyful tone and involve Team Leaders in one or all of these activities:

1. Tell one or more Bible stories using *Storytelling Leader Guide*.

2. Make a snack from the *Snack Leader Guide*.

3. Play a game from the *Game Leader Guide*.

4. Sing songs and do actions. Use the *Moovin' and Groovin' Passalong CD & DVD* or the *Song-Action DVD* with the *Good Times Music Leader Guide*.

Other Handouts for Team Leaders

If you do not involve Team Leaders in your volunteer training, share discipline guidelines and child-safety policies via handouts. See the section in the Team Leader Pages too. Make sure they have the following handouts and information:

- Expectations, including closing events, and emergency and first-aid information.

- Copies of a filled-in Team Chart from the *Director CD*. Add phone numbers and email addresses, if you have permission.

- Five *Sign In & Out Sheets* for each Team Leader (one sheet for EVERY LESSON) from the *Director CD*.

- A list of their kids and the people who are authorized to sign them in and out. If you don't have the lists done yet, tell the Team Leaders when they will receive them. Emphasize the importance of not releasing kids to unauthorized people or sharing the list information with anyone not on the VBS staff.

7. Safety!

It's important to find out if your church has policies about working with children. If child-protection policies are in place, make sure you understand them and have the resources to follow them. It may take time and money to follow procedures if you need to run background or criminal checks. State criminal checks can be run through your state highway patrol department. There are also companies specializing in national background checks. Determine if you need state or national criminal checks. The costs of these checks vary. Determine ahead of time how the background checks are financed. Your pool of volunteers may be limited if policies require volunteers to be a minimum age.

If you do not have child-protection policies, consider developing some with the help of your church staff and other volunteers. Contact the church's insurance company for policy development resources. Make sure your policies include working with parents to provide a safe learning environment for every child. Plan to recruit enough helpers so that children are well cared for and no adult is left alone with a child or children. This protects the volunteer as well as the child.

Once established, share the policies in writing at training sessions. Make sure everyone understands the policies and commits to following them. Follow the same procedure for discipline guidelines. Make sure to define steps to take if a problem arises.

Policy Examples

Here are some examples of child-protection policies to consider.

- Parents, volunteers, and church staff work together to give every child a safe place to learn and grow.
- No volunteer may work with children until he or she has been a church member for at least one year.
- The facility is clean and safe, and hazardous items have been removed.
- Two volunteers must be present at all times when working with children.
- No volunteer may be alone with children, especially in the restroom and when moving to different areas.
- Never send children to the restroom or another area alone or with other children.
- Children are treated with respect; the same is expected from them.
- Children are counted every time they move to a new area. Volunteers are responsible for each child in their small group.
- Even the appearance of impropriety must be avoided.
- Children must not be touched where a bathing suit covers.
- Parents and caretakers must sign children in and out each day.
- Children may be released only to adults listed on the registration form. If someone other than the parent is picking up the child that day, it should be noted on the sign-in sheet.
- Volunteers will be assigned to monitor child safety in the parking lot during arrival and departure.

Safety Training

In addition to protecting children from harmful people, you will need a plan in place to deal with dangers from emergencies such as fire, weather, intruders, or other crises. The children are likely unfamiliar with the evacuation and other safety plans for your church building. Though you probably don't need to host evacuation, shelter-in-place, or lockdown drills during VBS, a portion of your volunteer training should involve emergency awareness. Make sure evacuation routes are posted in each room you use for VBS and that volunteers are acquainted with those routes. Volunteers should know where fire alarms and fire extinguishers are located throughout your facility. Designate meeting areas away from your building for each Team to gather in case of an emergency. If you need assistance in planning fire escape routes or other fire safety issues, most local police and fire departments are more than happy to assist.

Severe weather safety should also be a concern for VBS Leaders. Purchase or borrow an inexpensive weather-alert radio, and keep it near your VBS administration area. Make sure volunteers know the location of the nearest shelter-in-place areas throughout your building. Walkie-talkies are useful for keeping in touch with Game Leaders or those who might be outdoors or away from your main gathering area during VBS.

Certain areas have additional safety risks, such as earthquakes, hurricanes, and so forth. Be sure to have plans in place and to train volunteers in dealing with these types of emergencies, if they are relevant to your region.

Emergency Phone Numbers

During an emergency, it's easy to become distracted; it is extremely important to have a list of important emergency phone numbers readily available ahead of time. If the phone system in your church requires dialing an additional number to connect with an outside line, make sure all volunteers know this information. Also, write the address of your building on the list.

Write each phone number clearly, including information about connecting to an outside line. As you create your own phone list, make sure it includes the numbers suggested here.

---

911 is the number for **fire**, **ambulance**, and **police** in most communities. State the emergency and be prepared to provide details, along with your name and the location of the emergency. **Stay on the line with the emergency dispatcher** for instructions and further questions.

1-800-222-1222 is the number for the **nationwide poison control center**. This toll-free number will connect you with the local poison control center.

Other Important Emergency Information:

_____

hospital emergency room

_____

fire department

_____

police department

_____

animal control

_____

electric company

_____

natural gas company

_____

location of your building

---

8. Promote, Publicize, Register!

Publicity Postcards 32-1609

Round Up Those Registrations!

Web Registration Flyer 32-1643

Publicity Poster 32-1693

Barnyard Roundup Indoor/Outdoor Banner 32-1610

Each minute you invest in publicity shows direct results in VBS registration. Good publicity increases preregistrations and lets you make more accurate decisions about supplies, space, snacks, and volunteers.

Remember, first impressions are lasting ones. Still, marketing experts say people need to hear or see information at least seven times before they respond. This becomes even more important when you consider the busy lives of families.

Decide whether you will use online or physical registration (or a combination). Concordia provides a free online registration tool! Find it at cph.org/vbsmate.

Use these suggestions to promote registration:

- **Announce VBS dates** early and often.
- **Publish VBS information** in church bulletins and newsletters six months ahead.
- **Send registration invitations** to member children and previous VBS attendees.
- **Place registration information** around your church; in neighborhood stores; and at doctor, dentist, and orthodontist offices.

- **Hand out registration information** at baseball games, parks, the library, the swimming pool, and other places where kids and their families go.
- **Take registrations** on your church's website, by phone, by mail, and at the church office.
- **Provide registration and invitation forms** so members can invite their friends.
- **Set up a VBS information table during weekend worship services.** If you use paper registrations, this is a great time to distribute and accept registrations.
- **Add children to your database** as registrations come in, so you can sort by both alphabetical order, age, and grade to prepare lists for registration day. (If you use our online registration, you'll be able to create reports with just the information you need.)
- **Follow guidelines of the Children's Online Privacy Protection Act (COPPA).** You can read more about COPPA at www.coppa.org.
- **Add the church's office number and email address to all publicity pieces.** Make sure the office has registration forms. Set up the phone answering system with a special VBS greeting to take messages when no one is in. Return calls promptly.

Publicity Planning

Choose your best publicity strategies, and list completion dates in order as a Publicity Plan. If you like, recruit a Publicity Coordinator to manage these efforts. Chart your strategies on the Publicity Plan on the *Director CD*.

Encourage children to invite their friends. Personal invitations are the most effective evangelism tool. Children know which of their friends go to church and which don't. They know which ones have questions about God. This knowledge makes children effective personal recruiters for VBS. Use these ideas to encourage children to bring friends to VBS.

1. **Talk to Sunday School children about inviting their friends to VBS two months prior.** Role-play a few ways to invite friends; have kids work in pairs to practice one or more of these ways. List things you can do to help friends feel welcome at church.

2. **Have Sunday School children write letters to invite their friends to VBS** one month prior.

3. **Ask the Sunday School to pray about VBS.** Ask God to use your VBS to bring children to hear about Jesus.

4. **Ask your Pastor to pray for VBS** at worship for several weeks.

5. **Welcome newcomers and recognize children who brought friends** during VBS.

Gather This Great Idea!

If you aren't using online registration, the Registration Form is on the *Director CD*. Print copies for duplication.

Letter to a Friend

Give a copy of the letter (right; also found on the *Director CD*), a piece of your church's letterhead, and a stamped envelope to children in your parish. Have kids copy the letter in their own handwriting to send to a friend they want to invite to VBS. Have the children address the envelopes too.

Hello, friend!

I'm going to Vacation Bible School, and I'd like you to come with me!

My church, (church name), is sponsoring Barnyard Roundup, a Vacation Bible School program on (dates) from (time) to (time).

At Barnyard Roundup, we'll learn about Jesus, our Savior, meet new friends, do fun activities, sing great songs, make crafts, play games, eat snacks, and more! It's going to be fun, but it would be more fun with you there.

Can you join me? Let's ask our parents to talk about getting us there.

Your friend,

(name)

Written Announcements

As you write and design publicity pieces, ask yourself, what information would I need if I knew nothing about VBS or this church?

Maximize publicity effectiveness with these strategies:

1. Announce VBS dates and times at least six months in advance.

2. Insert VBS registration information in worship bulletins every other week, starting two to three months before VBS. In the last six weeks, increase to weekly distribution.

3. Add brief notes in Sunday bulletins to encourage registration and to request prayers. Ask for needed donations, such as decorating items, snacks, and craft materials.

4. Send press releases to local newspapers and radio and TV stations (know their deadlines, article length, and photo requirements).

5. Paying for ads is expensive and offers little return.

Bulletin and Email Notes

We've created a series of bulletin notes that you can send to your Church Secretary. You fill in the local details, and she can cut and paste them into your church bulletins each week. The notes are found on the *Director CD*. Send them all at once and clearly note the dates when each note should be included in the church bulletin.

An email announcement for VBS is also on the *Director CD*. Send information about VBS to a list of email addresses from last year's VBS families, families in your congregation, and other addresses available to you.

Double-Check Data on Publicity Pieces

- Dates
- Times
- Church name and address, with map
- Ages of eligible children
- Activities and special features
- Online registration information
- Registration phone numbers
- Contact person's name and title
- Closing Program date and time

Attention Getters

Banners Attract! The *Outdoor Banner* gets attention. Personalize it with your program information.

Use the Decorating Posters! Mount the Theme Poster from the huge *Decorating Posters* on cardboard, and place it in your entry beside a registration table. Use the Registration Table Banner from another of the posters to draw attention to your table.

Hang Publicity Posters at church and community locations.

Farm-tastic Preview! Host an evening or daytime "barnyard" experience where members can gather 'round, enjoy a campfire, eat *Bountiful Blessing Snacks*, and get a preview of songs and games from *Barnyard Roundup*.

Floating! Make a float to advertise VBS in a summer parade. Use ideas from the "Decorate!" section or in the site descriptions. Enlist children to ride on the float and toss wrapped candies to the crowd. Have teens and adults walk alongside to hand out informational flyers.

Carnival with Petting Zoo! Set up a neighborhood carnival or block party with farm animals to pet and games for children. Recruit volunteers to staff a VBS information table with flyers and registration forms.

Invite a mall-full of children! Take *Polly the Pig Puppet*, other decorations, registration forms, and pens to a mall, shopping center, grocery store, or library. Set up a registration table, and sign kids up on the spot.

Post it! Ask business owners to hang VBS posters at their place of business.

Personal Invitations

Children love to get mail! Send VBS invitations to member children and past attendees. Send out invitations when the summer program information is released in your community, six to eight weeks before VBS, or certainly before school ends. Develop and maintain lists for future mailings.

Use friendly phrases such as "you are invited"; "a personal invitation"; and "meet new friends." Send the invitations from a person, not an institution. Add your name or your Pastor's name to the return address. Jot greetings to children you know personally.

Send invitations and VBS messages to parents' email addresses. The *Director CD* and Concordia's VBS website (vbs.cph.org) have ready-to-use or customizable theme emails you can use.

Telephone

Call congregation members and invite them to enroll their children. Personal contact develops a positive relationship between parents and program leaders, building a strong base for VBS and other congregation activities.

Make calls yourself, or recruit a Phone Coordinator and committee with great phone and relationship skills. Callers can make 15 to 20 calls in 30 minutes, if they stay on task. Call on evenings or weekends to catch people at home, but avoid mealtimes. Leave messages on answering machines if no one answers. Check back a week later if there's still no response.

When phoning, emphasize that you want to give members a chance to enroll before registration fills. You might say,

This is [your name] from church. I'm calling to ask you to enroll [children's names] in our *Barnyard Roundup* Vacation Bible School program this summer. We're expecting a record number of participants and want to make sure your child gets a chance to participate.

Provide details about the program if people are unfamiliar with VBS. Even if they do not enroll their children, you've reminded parents of their job to provide Christian education. You may also gain insight about scheduling conflicts that prevent people from attending.

Multimedia Resources

The *Farm-tastic Overview DVD* in the *Starter Kit* has several resources you can use to publicize VBS or recruit helpers, including a commercial to recruit volunteers and get kids to sign up. Some VBS Directors show the continuous-play version of the *Barnyard Roundup* Program Overview from the *Farm-tastic Overview DVD* so families can view it as they come and go to worship or church events. Others use it as part of registration information tables at a mall, neighborhood store, or church entryway.

Show the mission segment from the Lesson 1 Opening to church members to promote the Mission Project before VBS.

Make your own video or PowerPoint presentation for promotion or to use at a Closing Program. If you use pictures of children, make sure to get parents to sign a photo permission form. It's included with the Registration Form on the *Director CD*.

Farm-Tastic
Overview DVD

Registration Planning

Efficient registration planning makes VBS go better the first day and every day! Our convenient online tool captures consistent and complete enrollment while giving your community the convenience to enroll at any time or easily share with friends. Customize your own message, host up to three VBS-related events, create your own fields and reports—flexibility is yours. Tutorial videos are there when you need extra help. Publicity tools streamline your promotional efforts. Concordia's VBS Team is here to help at vbsteam@cph.org.

iStock/Thinkstock

Zip over to cph.org/vbsmate and start planning today!

cph.org/VBSMate   vbs.cph.org   800.325.3040

Assign Small Groups

When you are ready to assign your Teams, make three copies of the registration forms, organized alphabetically. One set should be given to your church office to hold for emergency response. One set should be kept as your master. One set will be used to create your class rosters.

Create a file folder for each Team Leader. This will be a simple way to make assignments. Attach the Attendance Sheet (provided on the *Director CD*) to the outside of the folder to make quick assignments and to create an attendance tracker for the Team Leader to use during VBS.

Once you decide how many preschoolers you can have in each Team, you'll need to determine whether to host mixed-age or same-age classes. Make a list of room assignments showing leaders' names. Add children's names as they register. Early Childhood Leaders will organize and manage small Teams of preschoolers for rotations.

We suggest assigning same-age or similar-age small groups. Use the form on the *Director CD*.

1. Sort registration forms for elementary kids into stacks, sorted by grades.

2. Assign each child to a Team with a Team Leader.

3. Leave two or more spaces in each Team for new arrivals. Six is the maximum number per group.

4. Make new Teams as needed. Stay flexible enough to make changes, if necessary.

5. Attempt to honor requests from children or parents to be in a Team with a friend.

6. Identify Teams by names or colors if you like. *Barndana Team Identifiers* come in five colors for this purpose.

Registration and Check-in Site at VBS

Registration and Check-in are two different activities for the first day of VBS. A registration table is needed for children who HAVE NOT yet registered for VBS and so have not been assigned to a Team.

A Check-in table or area is needed for students who HAVE ALREADY registered and been assigned to a Team.

If your VBS is under 50 students, Registration and Check-in could be handled with two tables side by side. If your VBS is larger than that, it is helpful to have the areas more physically separated and two distinct sets of volunteers—one set helping to get kids registered, and the other helping to get registered kids to their Teams (small groups) and signed in.

If you have a large VBS, consider offering separate Early Childhood and Elementary Check-ins. This allows preschoolers to have less anxiety about a strange place. However, consider how this setup might affect your volunteer staffing needs as well as the time required from parents for checking in children of varying age groups.

Check-in Preparation for the First Day of VBS

Take these actions to get ready for Check-in on your first day of VBS.

- Plan for one registration helper for every 40 preregistered children.

- Use extra helpers to escort kids and parents where they need to go and introduce them to Team Leaders. Ask these volunteers to arrive an hour before VBS starts.

- Compile a final list, alphabetized by last name, of all preregistered children, listing their Team and Team Leader assignments.

- Write a brief list of check-in procedures. Items may include check-off columns for check-in, medical/photo release form(s) received, and payment received.

- Make and copy facility maps to show the locations of Opening and Closing and also room and rotation assignments, especially noting drop-off and pick-up locations. Add information about your procedures for signing in and out.

- Prepare all letters or flyers that go home to families. The Parent Letter and the Introduction Letter are on the *Director CD*. Customize them for your local needs. You may wish to provide this information to each parent at check-in.

- Post signs for Check-in and Registration. See the *Director CD*.

Registration/Check-in Setup Details for First Day of VBS

Open Registration and Check-in 30–45 minutes before VBS starts.

- Post large signs in the parking lot and on outside doors to direct traffic to Check-in area.

- Designate separate tables for Check-in (for preregistered kids) and Registration (for walk-ins).
- Stock the tables with staplers, pens, blank nametags, and any other supplies.

Check-in
for Preregistered Kids

- At the Check-in area, divide the preregistered list into alphabetical ranges, such as A–H, I–M, and N–Z.
- Workers need to check off kids' names as they arrive.
- Provide check boxes for workers to indicate they captured or covered all the check-in procedures:
  - Small-group or room assignments, and how you are conducting drop-off and pick-up
  - Nametag provided
  - Registration form information complete
  - Medical/photo release form submitted
  - Registration fees paid, if applicable
  - T-shirt, *Moovin' and Groovin' Passalong CD & DVD*, Parent Letter, Mission Letter, or other items distributed, if applicable
  - Other notes specific to your local setup
- Ask registration helpers to escort students and parents to meet Team Leaders or Early Childhood Leaders.

Daily Student Check-in

Parents sign all children in and out of VBS daily with Team Leaders. Make sure Early Childhood and Elementary Team Leaders have the following information:

- A Sign In & Out Sheet for each day (on the *Director CD*)
- A list of children assigned to each leader and names of authorized signers

Before dismissal each day, update the pick-up lists with new attendees.

9. Closing Celebration!

Plan a Closing Program where children can tell their parents, relatives, and friends about Jesus, our Good Shepherd! Schedule the celebration when most adults can attend—perhaps a Thursday or Friday evening, or a Friday or Saturday morning. Include preschoolers in Closing Programs and weekend worship opportunities. Keep closing activities simple, brief, lively, and fun. Let children share music and activities, including Bible Memory Verses.

Introduce your Pastor and church staff members at closing events. Thank volunteers publicly and have appreciation gifts and the Volunteer Thank You Certificate (on the *Director CD*) filled out and ready to distribute. Recognize children's attendance with Student Certificates (on the *Director CD*). The *Director CD* has a ready-to-use but editable PowerPoint slide presentation for the Closing Program.

Showcase *Barnyard Roundup!*

Hosting a closing celebration and program is a great way to bring families together and to introduce visitors to members of your congregation. You'll know what's doable in your setting, but consider the following elements as you create a memorable event.

Hospitality

Provide informal socializing time before or after closing activities. Provide a *Barnyard Roundup* Picnic, and re-create the snacks in the *Snacks Leader Guide*. (Consider the "All Mixed Up" Snack Mix in Lesson 4.) Or you could set up different "create-a-snack" stations, where children could show their parents how they made the VBS snacks! Some programs offer a picnic or light meal before an evening program. Ask families to bring a contribution to a dessert buffet after the Closing Program.

Interactive Fun

Lead games for adults and children to do together from the *Game Leader Guide*. Teach a favorite song and its actions to the families.

Open House

Open your sites, and ask leaders to meet and greet families in their area. Invite children to give their parents tours. Display crafts. Invite members of your outreach or assimilation committee to attend so they can make important contacts with newcomers and interested families.

Closing Celebration

Gather everyone for a Closing Program in your Opening and Closing area. An outline for a VBS Closing Program is included on the following pages.

Publicize

Get the word out about your activities several weeks ahead of time in church publications and during VBS week in letters that go home to families. Invite the congregation to attend.

Closing Program—Why, Who, and How

The Closing Program is a great way to share VBS songs and to review the Bible stories, Memory Verses, and Take-Home Points from the week while the children show and teach their parents the things they have done. We've provided three items: a detailed script, a program outline based on the script, and a colorful PowerPoint presentation you can use and edit with your own VBS pictures and details! You can print copies of the program outline for those who attend, if you wish. All these items can be edited to create your unique program. (The *Barnyard Roundup* Closing Program Script, Closing PowerPoint, and Closing Program Outline are found on the *Director CD*.)

Involve Your Pastor

The Closing Program is the perfect place for your Pastor's visible involvement. Because you're likely to have a good number of visitors in the audience, VBS is an ideal opportunity for evangelism and witness. When the Pastor takes the lead in the event and the Closing Program, he is clearly identified. Visitors can connect with him and see your parish in action. When visitors return for a regular worship service, they'll be glad they know the Pastor.

Be sure to meet with your Pastor to go over the details and plans for the event. The *Pastor's Overview* has information about the Closing Program.

Involve the Children

The more the children can be part of telling their VBS story, the better! One easy way to get them involved is for different kids or Teams to narrate the various days, using the *Closing Program Script*. Children can sing the songs and recall the Bible Challenge Verses. Adapt it to suit your needs: add, cut, or rearrange!

The accompanying PowerPoint presentation is also completely editable, so you can add your local details. Be sure to include photos from your VBS!

If you have the time and ability, add to the program by inviting the Teams to "report" on aspects of the week. You could even act out a Bible story or two and recall the Bible Challenge activities.

Barnyard Roundup Closing Program

Find an outline version of the Closing Program on the *Director CD* to print programs for your closing celebration. The slide numbers refer to a PowerPoint presentation on the *Director CD*. There are slides where pictures from your local VBS can be inserted. As you customize the program, be aware that slide numbers will change from those in the script.

Welcome and Opening Prayer

SHOW SLIDE 1 (the *Barnyard Roundup* logo with title "Closing Program" on the screen).

Introduce your Pastor and yourself (each gives words of welcome).

Pastor will lead the Invocation and the prayer. **SAY**, In the name of the Father and of the Son and of the Holy Spirit. Amen.

PRAY, Lord Jesus, our Good Shepherd, You love us and gather us together as Your flock, the Church. Thank You for always being with us, providing for us, and protecting us now and forever. In Your name we pray. Amen.

Introduce *Barnyard Roundup*

SHOW SLIDE 2 (Add pictures from your VBS week!).

SAY, In *Barnyard Roundup* VBS, the children learned that Jesus, our Good Shepherd, gathers us together! We looked in the Bible, God's Holy Word, and explored five farm-tastic Bible accounts that teach us how God is with us, provides for all our needs, and protects us now and forever! Jesus, our Savior, cares, provides, leads, and forgives us! Now, we'd like to share our VBS with you!

SHOW SLIDES 3–12 (the words to "Always and Forever, No Matter What!").

CHILDREN SING "Always and Forever, No Matter What!"
PLAY *Music CD*, Track 1 or 20.
SHOW SLIDE 13 (additional pictures from your VBS week).

SAY, Our small groups, or Teams, started in Gather 'Round Opening. Then the Teams and their Team Leaders went to five sites: Storytelling, Bible Challenge, Snacks, Games, and Crafts. At each site, we heard that Jesus gathers us together! Check out these pictures!

(You may wish to add text related to your VBS or play an instrumental track of a favorite VBS tune as the pictures are shown.)

Tin Roofs for Africa (VBS Mission Project)

SHOW SLIDE 14 (slide about *Tin Roofs for Africa* Mission Project).

SAY, Through our Mission Project, *Tin Roofs for Africa*, we gathered together offerings to show the love and mercy of Christ by providing tin and other supplies for Lutheran church roofs in Africa. Then men, women, and children can have a better place to worship God and learn about the amazing love of Jesus—rain or shine! Specifically, our offering can provide tin for the roofs, wood for the church structure, nails, and toolboxes with hammers, saws, and other tools!

Early Childhood Kids and Polly the Pig

SHOW SLIDE 15 (Early Childhood Slide)

Have the Early Childhood Leader bring up *Polly the Pig Puppet.*

SAY, I'd like you to meet Polly the Pig. She was our helper in our Early Childhood program. Let's have the children come up and remind us about all of their adventures with Polly! Polly had just arrived at the farm, so it was fun to get to know her.

SAY, The first thing we found out was that she didn't have a name! She liked the name *Polly* so Polly she is! She was so excited when the farmer called her by name! Jesus said He is our Good Shepherd! Jesus knows our names. He loves and cares for us! Jesus is with us always!

SAY, Our second time together, Polly started wailing that she was HUNGRY! She didn't think the farmer cared and was going to feed her! We reminded her that the farmer has provided her with a nice pen with lots of mud. She loved her pen! Then she found out that the farmer was generous and gave her lots of food when it was feeding time. She had more than enough, so she shared with another pig named Perry! Jesus is generous too! He provides for all our needs, now and forever!

SAY, The next time, Polly found a hole in the fence. She looked through that hole and saw a field where she could run with the horse. She also saw watermelons she wanted to eat. We talked to her about staying in the pen and obeying the farmer. We also talked about the dangers on the other side of the fence. Polly didn't go through the hole, but Perry did. Polly was very worried about Perry.

Jesus, our Good Shepherd, provides for us and keeps us safe, now and forever. He leads us in paths of righteousness as we hear God's Word.

SAY, The fourth time we visited with Polly we heard about what happened to Perry. He had fun running with the horse. Then the horse left and Perry was all alone. He fell in a hole, heard wild animals, and finally got out of the hole, but he was all scratched up. He couldn't open the watermelons so he ate the rind and got a tummy ache! THEN, he got tangled up in the vines and got a sunburn! When Perry came back, the farmer made a big fuss over him and took care of him. We were glad that Polly stayed in the pen and that Perry is back. The farmer and the pigs all celebrated Perry's return!

In our Bible story, Jesus told a story about a man with two sons. One went off like Perry and finally decided that it was better to be at home! His father welcomed him back. God welcomes us back and forgives us when we sin. Jesus forgives us, now and forever.

SAY, During our last time together, we found out there was a bad storm. Polly didn't hear the farmer ringing the bell to come into the barn. Polly got stuck in the storm and hurt her ear on the fence. Then she heard the farmer calling her name. He found her and carried her back into the barn. Polly was so happy to have a farmer who loves and cares for her! He could have stayed in the barn where it was dry and safe, but he came out in the storm to rescue her!

Jesus knows our names. He died and rose again to rescue us from sin and Satan. Jesus is our Savior. He loves and cares for us, now and forever!

SAY, Now, the preschoolers will sing one of their songs!

Preschoolers sing one of the Early Childhood songs or another VBS song. The songs are on the *Music CD*. They are "God Is Near" (Track 14); "I Am Jesus' Little Lamb" (Track 15); "Love in a Box" (Track 16); "My Shepherd" (Track 17); "The Baa, Baa Song" (Track 18); and "We Plow the Fields and Scatter" (Track 19). (There are no instrumental versions for the Early Childhood songs.)

Lesson 1: Jesus Is the Good Shepherd

SHOW SLIDES 16–21 (with the words to "Have No Fear, Little Flock").

CHILDREN SING "Have No Fear, Little Flock."

PLAY *Music CD*, Track 6 or 25.

SHOW SLIDE 22 (Lesson 1 Take-Home Point).

SAY, Psalm 23 tells us that the Lord is our shepherd who is always with us. The Lord provides for us and protects us, now and forever! We learned about Psalm 23 in VBS through the Bible Stories we learned, the Bible Memory Verse activities we did, and the songs we sang! Jesus, our Good Shepherd, gathers us together in His flock, so we don't need to be afraid! Jesus cares! So, let's gather 'round and say our Take-Home Point!

Do the actions when saying the Take-Home Point as the children join you.

LEADER: GATHER 'ROUND! (Point up and circle hand.) **JESUS CARES!**

TEAMS: (Point up.) **JESUS CARES!** (Circle hand.) **NOW AND FOREVER!**

In "Jesus Is the Good Shepherd," Jesus taught the people who He was as He told them a story about a good shepherd. The shepherd came in to the fold by the door. The sheep knew the shepherd's voice and he called their names. They followed him. The shepherd kept them safe. Jesus, our Good Shepherd, cares for us.

SHOW SLIDE 23 (Lesson 1 Bible Challenge verse). You may wish to sing the verse instead (Track 9 or 28).

SAY, Our Green Pastures Bible Challenge verse is the first verse of Psalm 23! VBS kids, say (sing) it with me: "The LORD is my shepherd; I shall not want," Psalm 23:1.

Lesson 2: Jesus Feeds 5,000 People

SHOW SLIDES 24–31 (with the words to "Savior, like a Shepherd Lead Us").

CHILDREN SING "Savior, like a Shepherd Lead Us."

PLAY *Music CD*, Track 7 or 26.

SHOW SLIDE 32 (Lesson 2 Take-Home Point).

SAY, In "Jesus Feeds 5,000 People," Jesus and His disciples had gone away to rest, but people followed them. Lots and lots of people. The Bible says Jesus had compassion on them, because they were like sheep without a shepherd. He taught them many things. Late in the day, everyone was hungry and there was not enough food for so many people. Jesus had the people sit down on the green grass. Jesus took five loaves and two fish, gave thanks to God, and broke the loaves. He told the disciples to give the food to all the people. A miracle happened! Those five loaves and two fish fed all the people, and there were twelve baskets of leftovers! Jesus provided for the people who were hungry for God's Word AND hungry for food to eat!

Jesus provides for us too! He gives us food to eat, homes, and parents and others to care for us. Jesus died to pay for our sins and rose again to give us eternal life. Through His Word, God provides all we need to keep our faith strong and growing.

LEADER: GATHER 'ROUND! (Point up and circle hand.) **JESUS PROVIDES!**

TEAMS: (Point up.) **JESUS PROVIDES!** (Circle hand.) **NOW AND FOREVER!**

SHOW SLIDE 33 (Lesson 2 Bible Challenge verse). You may wish to sing the verse instead (Track 10 or 29).

SAY, Our Green Pastures Bible Challenge verse is—VBS kids, say (sing) it with me—"He makes me lie down in green pastures," Psalm 23:2.

Lesson 3: Jesus Tells about a Sower

SHOW SLIDES 34–45 (with the words to "All Together Come and Gather").

CHILDREN SING "All Together Come and Gather."

PLAY *Music CD*, Track 2 or 21.

SHOW SLIDE 46 (Lesson 3 Take-Home Point).

SAY, Jesus told a story about a farmer who was sowing seed all over his field. The seed landed on the path, on rocks, in thornbushes, and on good soil. When the seed landed on good soil, it grew and grew and produced a bountiful harvest! After Jesus told the story, He explained that the seed was like God's Word. God wants His Word to be shared all over! Jesus, working through God's Word, leads us in the paths of righteousness. God abundantly spreads His Word and provides the abundant and fruitful harvest.

LEADER: GATHER 'ROUND! (Point up and circle hand.) **JESUS LEADS!**
TEAMS: (Point up.) **JESUS LEADS!** (Circle hand.) **NOW AND FOREVER!**

SHOW SLIDE 47 (Lesson 3 Bible Challenge verse). You may wish to sing the verse instead (Track 11 or 30).

SAY, Our Green Pastures Bible Challenge verse is—VBS kids, say (sing) it with me—"He leads me in paths of righteousness," Psalm 23:3.

Lesson 4: Jesus Tells about a Lost Son

SHOW SLIDES 48–61 (with the words to "I Am a 'C'").

CHILDREN SING "I Am a 'C'."

PLAY *Music CD*, Track 5 or 24.

SHOW SLIDE 62 (Lesson 4 Take-Home Point).

SAY, In this lesson, Jesus tells a story about a father who had two sons. One son got all mixed up. He took his share of the property, left home, and spent everything. Then he had problems! He had no food, no home, nothing! He decided to go back home and ask his father for a job as a hired hand. BUT, his father had been waiting for him. He welcomed him home, forgave him, and celebrated with a party!

Jesus told the story to let us know that our heavenly Father loves us and forgives us for Jesus' sake! Jesus forgives us, gathers us together in His family, and gives us abundant life now and forever!

LEADER: GATHER 'ROUND! (Point up and circle hand.) JESUS FORGIVES!
TEAMS: (Point up.) JESUS FORGIVES! (Circle hand.) NOW AND FOREVER!

SHOW SLIDE 63 (Lesson 4 Bible Challenge verse). You may wish to sing the verse instead (Track 12 or 31).

SAY, Our Green Pastures Bible Challenge verse is—VBS kids, say (sing) it with me—"I will fear no evil, for You are with me," Psalm 23:4.

Lesson 5:
Jesus Appears to Mary in the Garden

SHOW SLIDES 64–77 (with the words to "He Is Risen").

CHILDREN SING "He Is Risen."

PLAY *Music CD*, Track 3 or 22.

SHOW SLIDE 78 (Lesson 5 Take-Home Point).

SAY, In the Bible account, "Jesus Appears to Mary in the Garden," after Jesus died on the cross, Mary went to the tomb on Sunday morning and found the stone moved. She told Peter and John. They ran to the tomb and looked in and saw only the grave cloths. The body of Jesus was not there! Then the two men went back to their homes. Mary stayed in the garden weeping. Jesus came up to her and asked, "Whom are you looking for?" Mary didn't recognize Jesus until He said her name, "Mary." At the sound of her name, Mary knew Jesus, her Teacher and Savior, was alive!

Jesus, our Savior, rescues us from sin, Satan, and death. We can't see Jesus bodily, but He is present in His Word and in the Sacraments. We can be confident He is always with us, and He knows our names—just as He knew Mary's.

LEADER: GATHER 'ROUND! (Point up and circle hand.) **JESUS IS OUR SAVIOR!**

TEAMS: (Point up.) **JESUS IS OUR SAVIOR!** (Circle hand.) **NOW AND FOREVER!**

SHOW SLIDE 79 (Lesson 5 Bible Challenge verse). You may wish to sing the verse instead (Track 13 or 32).

SAY, Our Green Pastures Bible Challenge verse is—VBS kids, **say** (sing) **it with me**—"I shall dwell in the house of the Lord forever," Psalm 23:6.

This is the last verse of Psalm 23, and we have a song that includes all the verses. We'll sing it for you now!

SHOW SLIDES 80–93 (with the words to "I Shall Dwell in the House of the Lord Forever").

CHILDREN SING "I Shall Dwell in the House of the Lord Forever."

PLAY *Music CD*, Track 4 or 23.

SHOW SLIDE 94. (Insert group photo of your VBS volunteers and candid shots of volunteers in action during the past week.)

SAY, We've had an awesome time with *Barnyard Roundup*! Jesus worked in and through the servant hearts of people to share His saving love! We thank the following . . . (Thank volunteers. You could list everyone by name as the PowerPoint slides are flashing.)

Closing Prayer and Benediction

SHOW SLIDE 95 (with the words to the prayer).

The Pastor leads the closing prayer and gives the Benediction.

PRAY, Dear Jesus, You are our Good Shepherd. Thank you. You take good care of us, provide everything we need, lead us, forgive us, and, through Your death and resurrection, You saved us. Jesus, gather us all together in Your flock so we will be with you, now and forever. In Your name we pray. Amen.

PASTOR SAYS, May God be gracious to us and bless us and make His face to shine upon us. Amen.

SAY, For our final song, let's sing "The Lord's My Shepherd, I'll Not Want."

SHOW SLIDES 96–102 (with the words to "The Lord's My Shepherd, I'll Not Want").

CHILDREN SING "The Lord's My Shepherd, I'll Not Want."

PLAY *Music CD*, Track 8 or 27.

Make any needed announcements before dismissing the group.

SHOW SLIDE 103 (the *Barnyard Roundup* logo).

Student Leaflets Are Essential at Barn Raising Storytelling

Farm Fresh Fun Elementary Leaflets

Scripture provided to read along in Storytelling and as a take-home piece.

Fun facts provide perspective and challenge.

Realistic Bible art communicates the authenticity of the Bible story.

Connection of Bible story elements with life application.

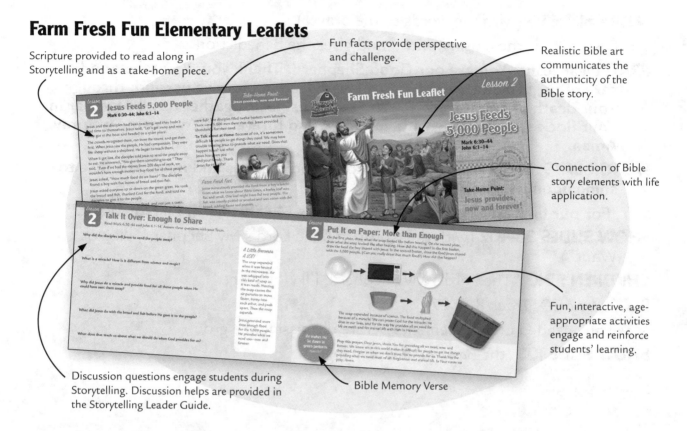

Fun, interactive, age-appropriate activities engage and reinforce students' learning.

Discussion questions engage students during Storytelling. Discussion helps are provided in the Storytelling Leader Guide.

Bible Memory Verse

Little Sprouts Early Childhood Leaflets

SONspot focuses on what God in Christ does for us.

Bible Memory Verse

Family Activities

Stickers included.

Fun, interactive, age-appropriate activities help reinforce teaching and engage students' learning.

Law and Gospel Connections

Jesus Cares, Now and Forever! Jesus gathers us and takes care of all our needs, now and forever. Together with the Father, He provides for all our needs of body and soul. He laid down His life for us, giving us salvation. Through the Holy Spirit, He takes care of us by protecting us from sin and Satan, gathers us together in His Church through Word and Sacrament, and leads us to everlasting life.

Law: Because of sin, we face physical and spiritual danger in this world; we can't take care of ourselves or live without God's care. We need Jesus.

Gospel: Jesus cares for us and gives us abundant life, now and forever.

Jesus Provides, Now and Forever! Through the power of the Holy Spirit, we know how caring Jesus is, trust in Him to provide for all our needs, and give thanks to Him for His abundant provision of "green pastures," now and forever.

Law: Because of sin, we face physical and spiritual danger in this world; we can't take care of ourselves or live without God's care. We need Jesus.

Gospel: Jesus abundantly provides all that we need for our bodies and our souls, now and forever.

Jesus Leads, Now and Forever! Jesus, working through God's Word, leads us in the paths of righteousness. God abundantly spreads His Word and provides the abundant and fruitful harvest.

Law: Our hearts are sinful, so we don't want to listen to or receive God's Word.

Gospel: Jesus leads us in the paths of righteousness and provides eternal life and salvation through the seed of God's Word.

Jesus Forgives, Now and Forever! Jesus forgives us, gathers us together in His family, and gives us abundant life, now and forever.

Law: We are sinners. We do what we want instead of what Jesus wants. We get in trouble.

Gospel: By His life, death, and resurrection, Jesus paid for our sins, redeemed us, and gives us eternal life. Jesus finds us and gives us forgiveness.

Jesus Is Our Savior, Now and Forever! Through the power of the Holy Spirit, by faith, we know and believe in our Savior, who achieved victory over death for us. Jesus calls us by name and gathers us to Himself, giving us salvation. We marvel at what Jesus has done for us, and we joyfully tell others the Good News that Jesus is our Good Shepherd who overcame sin and death.

Law: Without a Savior, we would remain in our sins. We are defenseless against our enemies of sin, death, and Satan.

Gospel: Jesus, the Good Shepherd of the sheep, is our Savior, now and forever. Jesus knows our names and calls us to be His own. He defends and protects us from our enemies. He laid down His life to save us. Because Jesus rose and is alive, we will have life in heaven.

We Want Your Feedback

We want to hear from you. Let us know what we did right, and help us learn where we can improve. Save time and postage by going online to www.cph.org/VBSfeedback. Please forward this link to all of your volunteers to ensure more comprehensive feedback. Online responses help us compile the results more efficiently and allow us to more quickly review your responses. You will find surveys for both the Director and the Volunteers at the link below. Thank you for your participation. Your feedback is valuable in helping us provide a VBS with Purpose!

www.cph.org/VBSfeedback

Volunteer Survey
Vacation Bible School

SAVE A STAMP and use the online form at cph.org/VBSfeedback

1. Name _____
   Address _____
   State/Province _____ ZIP/Postal Code _____
   Denomination _____
   State/Province _____ ZIP/Postal Code _____

Ministry Staff   ○ Pastor   ○ DCE   ○ Congregation Member   ○ Other

...w many years of VBS leadership experience do you have?
2–5   ○ 6–10   ○ 11–20   ○ 21+

○ Site leader at: or   ○ Helper at:
...sing   ○ Storytelling   ○ Bible Challenge   ○ Crafts   ○ Music
...dy   ○ Games   ○ Preschool   ○ Adult Bible Study   ○ Snacks
...pecify)

...Publishing House resources did you use in your role at VBS? (check all that apply)
...g Guide & DVD   ○ Music Leader Guide & CD   ○ Bible Challenge Guide & CD
...de & CD   ○ Elementary Leaflets   ○ Game Guide
    ○ Snack Guide   ○ Youth/Adult Bible Study
...e & CD   ○ Preschool Leaflets   ○ Other _____

...on of the resources you used?
...y to use   ○ Helpful but difficult to use
...not very helpful   ○ Difficult to use and not very helpful
...if _____

...on of the Volunteer Training site?
    ○ Helpful but needs more
    ○ Didn't know about it
...rces would help you on this site? _____

...es outside of the lesson plans?
..., please specify: _____

...these resources more helpful? _____

Director Survey
Vacation Bible School

SAVE A STAMP and use the online form at cph.org/VBSfeedback

1. Name _____
   Address _____
   City _____ State/Province _____ ZIP/Postal Code _____
   Email _____

2. Church Name _____ Denomination _____
   Church Address _____
   City _____ State/Province _____ ZIP/Postal Code _____
   Email _____

3. I am a . . . ○ Pastor   ○ DCE   ○ Children's Ministry Director   ○ Volunteer Director   ○ Other
   ○ Male   ○ Female   ○ 20–30   ○ 31–40   ○ 41–55   ○ 56+

4. What date(s) did you host VBS? ____ / _____ / ____
   In what month did you decide which VBS program to use? _____

5. What is the format of your VBS?   ○ 1 week, mornings   ○ 1 week, evenings   ○ 1 week, full day
   ○ Backyard camp   ○ Weekend   ○ One-day   ○ Other _____

6. How many children did you host at your VBS?
   ○ 0–24   ○ 25–49   ○ 50–99   ○ 100–199   ○ 200–499   ○ 500–999   ○ 1000+
   This was (circle one)   **greater than**   **less than**   last year by about this many: _____

7. How many children came from outside your church membership/regular attendees?
   ○ 0–24   ○ 25–49   ○ 50–99   ○ 100–199   ○ 200–499   ○ 500–999   ○ 1000+

8. How many volunteers did you have at your VBS?
   ○ 0–9   ○ 10–19   ○ 20–49   ○ 50–99   ○ 100–249   ○ 250+

9. What are the age ranges of the students you serve (lowest age to highest age)?
   preschool: ages ____ to ____   **elementary:** ages ____ to ____
   youth: ages ____ to ____ (youth VBS, not volunteers)   **adults:** ages ____ to ____ (adult VBS, not volunteers)

10. How did teens participate in your VBS? (Check all that apply.)
    ○ Students   ○ Team (small-group) leaders   ○ Site leaders   ○ Site assistants   ○ Other _____

11. Please share with us your favorite *Barnyard Roundup* memory or special comments you received from attendees.
    _____
    _____
    _____
    _____
    _____

Alphabetical List of VBS Enrollees

Name	Age	Grade	Group Leader	Day 1	Day 2	Day 3	Day 4	Day 5
				☐	☐	☐	☐	☐
				☐	☐	☐	☐	☐
				☐	☐	☐	☐	☐
				☐	☐	☐	☐	☐
				☐	☐	☐	☐	☐
				☐	☐	☐	☐	☐
				☐	☐	☐	☐	☐
				☐	☐	☐	☐	☐
				☐	☐	☐	☐	☐
				☐	☐	☐	☐	☐
				☐	☐	☐	☐	☐
				☐	☐	☐	☐	☐
				☐	☐	☐	☐	☐
				☐	☐	☐	☐	☐
				☐	☐	☐	☐	☐
				☐	☐	☐	☐	☐
				☐	☐	☐	☐	☐

Index